POETRY COM

CW00523839

GREAT MINDS

Your World...Your Future...YOUR WORDS

From The Midlands
Edited by Sarah Marshall

 Young**Writers**

First published in Great Britain in 2005 by:
Young Writers
Remus House
Coltsfoot Drive
Peterborough
PE2 9JX
Telephone: 01733 890066
Website: www.youngwriters.co.uk

SB ISBN 1 84602 070 0

Foreword

This year, the Young Writers' 'Great Minds' competition proudly presents a showcase of the best poetic talent selected from over 40,000 up-and-coming writers nationwide.

Young Writers was established in 1991 to promote the reading and writing of poetry within schools and to the youth of today. Our books nurture and inspire confidence in the ability of young writers and provide a snapshot of poems written in schools and at home by budding poets of the future.

The thought, effort, imagination and hard work put into each poem impressed us all and the task of selecting poems was a difficult but nevertheless enjoyable experience.

We hope you are as pleased as we are with the final selection and that you and your family continue to be entertained with *Great Minds From The Midlands* for many years to come.

Contents

Bablake School, Coventry

Kenny Sangha (12)   44
Amandeep Mankoo (12)   45
Oliver George (12)   46
Emily Mason (12)   47
Vikki Jones (12)   48
Ashleigh Lafaurie (11)   48

Beauchamp College, Oadby
Selina Khan (15)   49

Bristnall Hall Technology College, Oldbury
Elizabeth Ormston (11)   49
Zoe Hunter (13)   50
Emma Hall (15)   51
Marie Evans (14)   52
Suzi Jones (12)   53
Megan Price (12)   54
Charlotte Nicholls (12)   54
Charlie Higgins (13)   55
Zoe Wood (12)   55
Paige Boswell (12)   56
Charlotte Cash (13)   57
Holly Henderson (11)   58
Sandeep Gahir (11)   59

Codsall Community High School, Wolverhampton
Kate Jewkes (14)   59
Ryan Dil Sodhi   60
Stephanie Evans (13)   60
Hannah Kendall (13)   61

Derby Grammar School, Derby
Charlie Newport (15)   62

Hillcrest School, Birmingham
Sophie Cohen (12)   63
Natalie Bruce (11)   63
Paris Sanders (11)   64

Mehak Tariq (11)   65
Karina Binning (11)   65

Kings Langley School, Kings Langley

Natalie Maclean (14) & Katie Elkins (13)   66
Anna Mildner & Emma Parkinson (13)   66
Adam Hurn (13)   67
April Clarke (13) & Jenny Brooks (14)   67
James Witterick (14)   68
Richard Allen (14)   68
Warren Oakins, Christopher Malcolm
         & Daniel Pischedda (14)   69
Naomi Elaine Sadiq & Lilli Swaffield (13)   69
Iona Preston (14)   70
Grace King (14)   70
Caroline Hardingham (14) & Rebecca Davies (15)   71

Langley High School, Oldbury

Ciara Parsons (13)   71
Cherie Ellie Whyte (12)   72
Scott Bird (12)   73
Adam Overton (14)   74
Naomi Hughes (12)   74
Samantha Farrissey (14)   75
Micha Grosha (13)   75
James Hewitt (14)   76
Gemma White (12)   77
Lauren Waldron (12)   78
Katie Louise Hillyer (14)   79
Kerry Dalton (14)   80
Louise Thomson (12)   81
Matthew Skeldon (14)   82
Francesca Joanne Holden (14)   83
Benjamin Thomas Marshall (14)   84
Matthew Hawkes (14)   85
Alexandra Hoult (14)   86
Harinder Dhadda (14)   87
Nichola Stephanie Thompson (14)   88
Krizia Mills (14)   88

Pensnett School of Technology, Brierley Hill

Hayley Cooper (15)	89
Katie Winwood (15)	89
Becky Betts (14) & Natalie Fellows (15)	90
Melissa McGregor (15)	90
Aimee Garratt (14)	91
Zoe Nock (14)	91
Stephanie Jones (14)	92
Kelly Morris & Jade Checketts (14)	92
Susan Marsh (15)	93
Sam Cooper (11)	93
Lucy Ashley (14)	94
Jessica Bagley (14)	94
Samantha Williams (14)	95
Richard Marshall (11)	95
Aimée Tibbetts (11)	96
Shane Bennett (12)	96
Stevie Davies (11)	97
Suman Chauhan (12)	97
Liam Guest (12)	98
Zoë Westwood (11)	98
Sian Compton (11)	99
Stacie Boswell (11)	99
Jade Field (12)	100
Rebekah Gallimore (11)	100
Alexandra Shevlin (12)	101
Charlie Joanna Craig (11)	101
Emma Dalloway (11)	102
Paige Grosvenor (11)	102
Laura-Jade Morgan (11)	103
Lisa Marie Rowley (12)	103
Callum Giles (11)	104
Amy Sankey (11)	104
Sarah Smallwood & Mary Hall (12)	105
Gemma Louise Bolton (11)	105
Ali Tahir (12)	106
Kerry Roper (11)	106
Daniel Mallen (12)	107
Aaron Moore (11)	107
Kayleigh Woodall (11)	108
Chloe Jade Wood (11)	108

Sam Barnbrook (12)   153
Brett Wood (12)   153

Perryfields High School, Oldbury
Jay-Dee Johnson (15)   154
Jamie Coleman (13)   155
Louis Bridges (13)   156
Rachael Elizabeth Healey (13)   157

Queen Mary's High School, Walsall
Carly-Marie Talbot (14)   157
Ramanpreet Kaur Jassel (15)   158
Samantha Johnson (15)   159
Stephanie Jackson (16)   160
Charlotte Askew (17)   161

Ridgewood High School, Stourbridge
Samuel Archer (11)   162

Waseley Hills High School, Birmingham
Lucy Pilkington (12)   162
Aimee Bates (12)   163

Whiteheath Pupil Referral Unit, Rowley Regis
Adam Richards (15)   163
Jane Farmer (15)   164
Matthew Miccolls (15)   164
Alicia Biggs (15)   165
Stephen Brooks (15)   165

William Bradford Community College, Earl Shilton, Leicester
Samantha Marston (14)   166
Ruth Shred (14)   166
Craig Lawson (14)   167
Lucy Hyde (14)   167
Stephen Blighton (14)   168
Chloe Golding (14)   168
Jake Hines (14)   169
Nicholas Ordish (14)   169

Danielle Thorne (14)	195
Oliver Broad (15)	195
Amy Cox (14)	196
Amy Mitchell (14)	196
Kim Domican (15)	197
Ashley Woodley (14)	197
Matt Lawrenson (14)	198
Nina Marvin (14)	199
Hannah Maloney (14)	199
Kaitlin Duckworth (14)	200
Paige Steane (14)	200
Sophie Gent (14)	201
Amy Lymn (14)	201
Yvette Aspin (14)	202
Ashleigh Newell (14)	202
Helen Mayne (15)	203
James Sweeney (14)	203
Mallory Thorpe (14)	204
Laura Houghton (14)	204
Mathew Smith (14)	205
Siobhan Hanson-Spence (14)	205
Laura Di Salvo (15)	206
Holly Beasley (14)	206
Billy Mitchell (14)	207
Nicola-May Mangham (14)	207
Hayley Billington (14)	208
Katie Middleton (14)	208
Tom Holdsworth (14)	209
Adelle Armstrong (14)	209
Robyn Mains (14)	210
Jessie White (14)	210
Sarah Harding (14)	211
Charlotte Grewcock (14)	211
Scott Christopher (14)	212
Adam Farmer (14)	212
Emily Bates (14)	213
Rebecca Gault (14)	213
Kirsty Grewcock (14)	214
Florence Powers (14)	214
Emma Hogg (14)	214
Todd Astill (14)	215
Ben Lester (14)	215

The Poems

Who Is That Person In The Mirror?

There is a person in my mirror
Who looks just like me
Every day I see her
But who can it be?

I asked my mum
But she doesn't know
I wonder if she is my twin
But she can't be
There's only one of me.

Everything I do
She copies me
I tell her to go away
So she somehow says it back to me.

She is always there every day
This girl just like me
No matter what I do or say
She will never go away.

Chelie Stockbridge (11)

My Cat

My cat is black and sleek.
Its fur shines in the moonlight.
And eyes whistle as they leap.

Its claws are sharp and long, white and powerful
As they glide through the sand.
It plays and plays until the sun goes down
Across the ocean shore.

It drops painfully onto the blanket beneath the buried sand.
Its feet are weak and have no strength to move.
But poor little pussy lies there without a sound.

Harneel Paul (11)
Arden School, Solihull

Encore! Encore!

Dance like nobody's watching you,
and make us all proud, the stage,
the lights and the people in the crowd,
struck with fear, drowned in nerves,
watching my spins and my swerves.
Soon be over, but my one chance to
shine, I can't believe I dance so
fine. Wait! My mind just went
blank, I feel like I've jumped in a river
and sank. I'm on the front row as well,
as my family and friends watch as I
fail. I'm back on track with lots
of energy, my ears tingle as I hear
the soft melody. The curtain draws
as I hear the applause. Encore!
Encore! The crowd wants more!

Laura Crossley (12)
Arden School, Solihull

Food Poem

Chew, chew, munch, munch
When will it be time for lunch?

Pies, sausage, chips and peas
More for me, please, please, please!

Food is fun, food is great
More and more, fill up my plate.

Health and fitness not my goal
Bread and mash will fill my hole.

Eat your food, eat it now
It will give you lots of power.

Now some sweet custard, cake and cream
Thanks to the catering team!

Sarah Privett (12)
Arden School, Solihull

Dolphin Joy

Smooth and grey they glide towards me
Full of wonder of what might be.

Their glistening eyes and sharp, pointed fins,
Their long, shiny noses and wonderful grins.

My heart pounds with excitement as I rise above the sea,
I squeal with delight and my face lights up with glee.

As I fly up in the air and over the spray,
My two friendly dolphins, take me back to the bay.

As we head back to the shoreline, I feel so elated,
They gave me a kiss, if only they knew the joy they'd created.

Rosie Neville (11)
Arden School, Solihull

The Circus

Performers nervous to go on stage.
Lions ready in their cage.

Ringmaster standing with the light on him.
Suddenly the lights go dim.

He starts to speak, the people seek.
The juggler's race on with fire,
As the audience look on and admire.

They all look around with oohs and aahs.
The clowns drive on in their cars.

Acrobats swing high and low.
Tightrope walkers ready to go.
They're having fun running around,
They're all making one huge sound.

When you see a funny clown.
The circus is, of course, in town.

Elizabeth M Parry (13)
Arden School, Solihull

Black And White

Black and white
Used to fight
Due to different skin colour
The whites said black was duller
Different buses they were forced to catch
Because their skin colour didn't match
Different schools they were made to go
Whites didn't want black, you know
Treated badly, swept away
I'm ashamed of whites today
Martin Luther King realised
Why should the black be penalised?
He tried to rescue the black
Only to be shot dead in the back
We will always remember and know
Martin Luther King was a hero
But Nelson Mandela, a hero too
He showed the world what to do
He told the world to make amends
So then black and white could be friends
Black and white are better today
Most of the problems have gone away
Now the blacks can have a day
Now the blacks can have a say.

Sarah Hancox (12)
Arden School, Solihull

Grandparents Make Sense

The sound of knitting needles clicking
The smell of sweets in a handbag
The sight of their clashing clothes
The taste of yummy roast dinners
The touch of the many presents they give me
I love my grandparents!

Ellie Stamp (11)
Arden School, Solihull

All About Myself

My name is Kiran Kang,
And I live in a big house
With five bedrooms and a large garden,
Outside at the back lives a mouse
That sometimes looks like the character Marge.

I have a mum and dad,
Who sometimes get mad
And I have a granddad and granny,
Plus I have a brother
Who sometimes gets on my nerves.

On the outer family,
I have three aunts and four uncles
And roughly I have about nineteen cousins,
So what else do you really want to know, hey?
So maybe you can decide on what to say.

I hope you know a bit about me
And I hopefully will learn a bit about
You!

Kiran Kang (11)
Arden School, Solihull

The Winter Morning

Outside I am in the winter breeze
Standing there too long, start to freeze
All around me a big, white sheet
So silky soft, cold but neat
Picking up handfuls, more and more
Getting really cold now, run in my door
Mum shouts, 'Charlotte, hot chocolate's ready,'
Down the hall I run, steady
Walk into the kitchen, sit on my seat
And tuck into my warm, hot, tasty treat.

Charlotte Brookson (11)
Arden School, Solihull

Food For Thought

I went into the supermarket,
Going to get the weekly shop.
Couldn't help but stop and think,
Where does all that food come from?

Into the basket for Monday's tea,
Went spicy Mexican corn chips.
(My favourite are the cheesy ones,
Where the flavour covers your lips.)

For Tuesday we found the ingredients,
To make a healthy salad.
To make it like the Greeks,
We got loads of olives and feta.

On Wednesday we're having burgers,
With the buns from USA,
They are so unhealthy,
The fat must be weighed in tonnes!

For the week's breakfast,
We went into the bakery.
I chose some chocolate croissants,
Just like the ones we had in Paris.

We were heading straight for the till,
To pay for all the shopping,
When I paused and thought of all the work,
That went into every meal.

I thought I must be stupid,
To not even try to say thanks,
For all the food we love,
When some people don't get a chance.

Katie Evans (12)
Arden School, Solihull

The Ever-Wandering Storm

Here I am all alone,
Crouching on a milestone.
The rain comes pouring down,
But I just sit here all alone.
I hear the thunder clash and bang,
The lightning comes down in a long, scary fang.
Then more lightning comes down in a hurled bolt,
Most destruction is all its fault.
I feel so scared, I'm all alone,
Crouching on a milestone.
The grey clouds seem to swallow me,
All that I can do is scream.
A thunder clash surrounds the air,
But then I hear it disappear.
Moving away the sky is clear,
The storm is now not here.
The sun comes out and all is well,
I escaped the living Hell.
But I'm still here all alone,
Crouching on a milestone.

Andrew Farquhar (11)
Arden School, Solihull

The Sun

The sun is a ball of fire,
That burns you in the day.
The sun lets us see the moon,
And guides you in the day.
It's a street light in the sky,
But, oh how extremely high!
You sit in the sky,
Shining down onto Earth,
From that height, oh how high.

Alex Bleby (11)
Arden School, Solihull

The Happy Ending

Ted was bored so he said to his mum,
'Are we nearly there 'cause I'm not having much fun?
D'you know I really hate just driving in the car,
So are we nearly there or is it very far?'

For the hundredth time, Ted's mum replied,
'Not long now.' But had she truly lied?
As that is one of the things that Ted's mum would say,
When they were in the car travelling on holiday.

When Ted was in the car, it always seemed to rain,
But Ted's mood on the journey seemed to be the same,
The engine kept on droning and the rain was pouring down,
While Ted's face was contorted like a drowsy lion's frown.

But all the pain was worth it when they reached their destination,
For total joy and happiness was Cornwall's best creation,
The bliss of shimmering sand, in between your toes,
Makes you forget an irksome journey, no matter how it goes!

Jonathan Cunliffe (12)
Arden School, Solihull

Life In Darkness

The sky was as dark as black, thick smoke,
The trees were shaking around, rustling,
There was silence,
Then I heard the sound of dogs howling like a flute.

The leaves on the ground felt as rough as Astroturf,
The trees were rough stones,
It was cold.
It was dark.
It was scary.
It was horrible!

Matthew Baldock (11)
Arden School, Solihull

The Diary

I am the heart of silent screams,
I am the home of fears she writes,
I am the soul of stolen dreams,
The crying thought of darkened nights,
Blue from ink pours into me,
Makes my body filled with thoughts,
I am for no eyes to see,
For in her mind's great web I'm caught.
Tears even stain my pages,
Always joy rings through my words,
A million hopes all trapped in cages,
That no one saw and no one heard.
I am the heart of silent screams,
I am the home of fears she writes,
I am the soul of stolen dreams,
The crying thoughts of darkened nights.

Eleanor Barton-Mather (11)
Arden School, Solihull

Foxes!

Walking down the winding street
Hearing the foxes' fiery feet.

Hearing the foxes in the bins
Hearing the clattering of metal tins.

The white tip of their long, bushy tails
Following the foxes footprint trail.

Through the wood into the dark
Passing the other animals in their path
To their den to eat their meal
Ripping it apart with their baring teeth.

After their meal they lie down to rest
Curling up together in their nest.

It's a fox's life.

Lucy Ainsley (11)
Arden School, Solihull

My Cat

My cat is called Lucky,
He sleeps on my bed each day,
Then prowls around at night,
Catching all his prey.

Sometimes he is oh, so cute,
Or he'll scratch and bite,
And go outside to find,
A cat to pick a fight.

He cries to be let in and out,
And makes so much sound,
But when you stroke him,
He will purr, so I have found.

Chicken is his favourite food,
He'd eat it every day,
He doesn't get it all the time,
Even though he'd pay.

He's cuddly and fluffy,
And his fur is jet black,
Although he is large,
Doesn't mean he's fat.

But the most important fact,
Is that Lucky's *my* cat!

Rosie Bishop (11)
Arden School, Solihull

Night

Whispering shadows call from below
The time of night will now unfold
Ever closer, ever near
The time of night will soon be here.

Watch the mist reel in the night
The glinting eyes, a haunting sight
Ever closer, ever near
The cold of night is finally here.

The sunlight burns through the sky
The night is fading, how I sigh
Ever closer, ever near
The light of day will soon be here.

The night is fading, I see the day
Now it's time for night to pay
Ever closer, ever near
The dawn of day will soon be here.

Broken-hearted, forever lost
Now it's time to lose the frost
Ever closer, ever near
Now this night will disappear.

Conor Smith (11)
Arden School, Solihull

Through The Attic

Walking up the stairs one by one
Running an errand for my mum.

Onto the landing, pull down the ladder
Clamber up the tiers
And into the attic.

My head pokes through
And suddenly I hear a bang.
'It's just the thunder outside,' I tell myself.

I slowly walk to the back of the attic
Searching for the box.

It is quite dark back here
So I have to feel my way.
My fingertips curl around a handle.
Cautiously I twist it.

Bright, sunny light fills the attic and a tropical scent
Is carried on the gentle breeze.
I gingerly take an amazed step forwards
And feel sand under my feet!
Bright butterflies flicker by
And sprays of vivid flowers hang overhead.
Palm trees casually lean over, dripping with bananas.
I have found my very own tropical island!

Katherine Argent (11)
Arden School, Solihull

Winter

The trees were covered with icicles like crystals
The sky covered in an ocean of stars
The icy haze covered the air, still and quiet
The scent of fresh pine needles floating by
Log fires fill the air with a warm glow
Then it begins to snow . . .

Sacha Thorne (11)
Arden School, Solihull

The Last Warrior

A battle rages on and on,
Blood wipes out with a Ruby tongue,
A blade as sharp as a high note sung,
Wipes around under a crimson sun,
Many fall once it comes.
As many load blackened guns,
A man he runs, he runs,
Run, man, run,
Run for your life,
Run for your freedom.
Into the dreary wood he goes,
Where water red as blood flows,
And fragmented light shines and shows,
That few, yes, few knows,
The secrets that it beholds.
Not far but near,
Here they come,
With pitchforks, shovels and other weapons.
He jumps on a boat and rows and rows,
But alack and alas,
They shoot him with lead and powder,
With iron and wood,
The end has come,
The last warrior has fallen.

Samuel Phasey (11)
Arden School, Solihull

Fall

L et them fall
E ver twirling
A fter each other
V ery slowly
E very one
S oftly landing.

Lucinda Osbourn (12)
Arden School, Solihull

Old Age

It's hard to remember
How it was in your youth
Sound in your body
And strong in your tooth.

Now you are older
And your legs aren't so sure
They know what they're doing
But you wish they did more.

If you're lucky your brain
Retains all of its power
If you're not it can seem
Like you're locked in a tower.

But you must not despair
At your prospect of age
It can be a freedom
And not a dark cage.

With your years of knowledge
And your sense of what's right
You have so much to offer
To those who need insight.

You can guide and advise
The young of today
Who are just setting out
And making their way.

And your family is there
As you grow old and wise
To overcome your trials
And keep love in your eyes.

Emma Taberner (11)
Arden School, Solihull

Summer Morning

The air around was amazingly bright
And full of prancing specks of light
Butterflies were dancing too
Between the shimmering green and blue,
I may not go, I may not stay.

The straggling vines caught my feet,
The poppy field was oh, so sweet
I heard a singing in the sky
As soft as silk it glided by
And how I cannot tell
But everything around me sang as well.

Along the poppy field I ran
To where my little dream began
And there I stood free at last
And on that leaf of that very twisting tree
A fairy sat and smiled at me!

Elizabeth Austin (11)
Arden School, Solihull

Pink

Pink is the best,
Better than the rest.

Better than blue
Or purply goo
That's my opinion.

It is girly
And it's not very boyish.

But . . . that's why I like it.

It's *pink,* it's *pink*
That's what it is!

Emma Wilson (11)
Arden School, Solihull

I Remember

I am old,
Not very bold,
Some call me mad,
But I am glad,
To be as old as I can be,
If I could I'd dance with glee,
But here I am in my rocking chair,
Wondering what happened to my hair,
I'm trying to sleep, can't you see?
Please stop pestering me,
I'm sorry that I'm so grumpy,
Just go away and leave me be,
Are you still here,
My little dear?
Make yourself useful and put the kettle on,
I'll have two sugars and some jam on a scone,
Sit down by me,
And I'll tell you a story,
About,
ZZZZZzzzzzzzzzzzzzz . . .

Alistair Aktas (11)
Arden School, Solihull

The Sands

The sand is grainy and warm.
The sands are all over the world.
The sand is golden and yellow.
The sands are beautiful with shining grains.
Oh beautiful sand.
Miles and miles of sand.
So much of it.
Oh beautiful sands.

Sam Ellison (11)
Arden School, Solihull

Being Old

Their faces may get wrinkled
But there is a twinkle in the eye
They very often smile at me
When they pass me by.

Flowery dresses and a feather in their hat
Is what they seem to wear
The summery smell of perfume
And their blue-rinsed hair.

They have a lot of memories
And stories to be told
Most of them are fun to be with
Some are just grumpy and *old!*

Eventually we all grow old
And some may find that sad
But I just hope when it happens to me
That it won't be all that bad.

Lucy Wood (11)
Arden School, Solihull

The Wind

It was howling outside
My window was shaking.
The sounds in my garden
That the wind was making.

Trees were bending and swaying
The acorns fell onto the ground.
I went outside and the wind was so loud
You could not hear another sound!

As I looked up I saw clouds racing over
With the wind pushing behind them.
As I saw the great, dark clouds
I ran inside with a leap and bound.

Daniel Bloomer (12)
Arden School, Solihull

What Is It Like Getting Old?

No one likes getting old,
Or at least that's what I'm told.

Wrinkly skin, greying hairs,
Walking slowly up the stairs.

Going deaf, failing sight,
Getting frightened in the night.

But wait a minute, don't be sad,
Getting old is not all bad.

Retired from work, with time to spare,
Freedom to travel without a care.

Free bus passes and a pension,
'Discount Wednesdays' not to mention.

What will you think when you're old?
Maybe not quite what we're told.

Katharine Gough (11)
Arden School, Solihull

My Poem

The silence of night,
The deadly sight.
The mist and fog,
Me and my dog.
We got outside,
To see the fight,
Between mist and night.

I heard a noise,
I went nearer and nearer,
It might have been my dog,
It might have been a snore,
Then I saw it, a tree on the floor.

George Cole (11)
Arden School, Solihull

Snowflakes

Snowflakes, snowflakes floating down
Floating, floating to the ground
Covers the earth in a gleaming white
That's shining, shining, shining bright.

Snowflakes, snowflakes floating down
Floating, floating to the ground
Beautiful, fluffy flakes of snow
Over the woods and fields they go.

Snowflakes, snowflakes floating down
Floating, floating to the ground
Now everywhere I always play
Looks like somewhere else today.

Snowflakes, snowflakes floating down
Floating, floating to the ground.

Iona McIntyre (12)
Arden School, Solihull

Stormy Weather!

Thunder, lightning
Scary and frightening
Thunder cracking and creeping
Lightning waking you up from your sleeping!

Wind and rain
They give you pains in your brain
Wind blowing with might
Rain pouring through the night!

Hail and sleet
Make you cold in your feet
Hail, fast-flowing balls of ice
Sleet, cold, wet and not very nice!

Amy-Jane Sutheran (11)
Arden School, Solihull

Don't Call Me Old

I'm a wise old owl
Stuck in my tree
Hibernating all year long
I don't get out anymore
'Cos my wings are sore
And the feeling in my feet long gone.

I just totter around
Getting the tea
While my family come to visit me
But can I ask you just one favour . . .

Don't call me old
Call me older.

'Cos I'm a wise old owl
Stuck in my tree
And I've seen much more
Than you'll ever see.

Vanessa Scott (11)
Arden School, Solihull

Dogs

Dogs are like people, warm and friendly,
Cuddling up on the sofa, loving and tenderly.

A dog is like a person giving,
A very beautiful thing that its living.

Dogs protect their owners,
Like people protect their young.

Dogs are playful like babies,
They don't stop playing all day long.

People love their dogs,
Like dogs love their owners.

Charlotte Brearley (12)
Arden School, Solihull

Old People

Old people are experienced in life
They know the do's and don't's
They also can be kind, loving and understanding
But sometimes they can be a moody old grouch.

Old people are very different from the young generation
They know and understand
They also have a stash of sweets
Hidden away for you to find.

Old people treat you with respect
Well, most of the time
I like old people when they're kind, loving,
Understanding, thoughtful and caring.

Josie Harris (11)
Arden School, Solihull

The Wind

I'm cold,
Have no soul,
I'm very breezy,
No one sees me,
I come roaring through the towns,
Crash into their faces, see their frowns,
No one knows who I am,
Here's a clue, I don't live in a pram,
Everyone judges me,
Even though they cannot see,
I cause disasters in people's lives,
Churning and frothing, the oceans rise,
Trees uprooted, power lines down,
All you can hear when you stand around,
Is thud, crash, smack, clatter,
Down onto the ground.

Peter Blackhall (11)
Arden School, Solihull

Battle

Look at it
Just there, like no other
Reaching, twisting, straining to get a breath of sun.

Growing now
Quickly, ever reaching
Never getting any closer
But wrestling with the ground to let it free
It will never happen, it is in vain
A strong punch from the wind
Flies its darlings high into the air
The battle is over
A cold chill runs through its veins
Oh well, there is always next year
To grow a plant.

Owain Barratt (11)
Arden School, Solihull

The Sea Can Be Many Things

The sea is blue,
The sea is green,
The sea is many colours.

The sea has dolphins,
The sea has whales,
The sea has many animals.

The sea can be happy,
The sea can be sad,
The sea can be many moods.

The sea can be rough,
The sea can be calm,
The sea can be many things.

Kate Ellison (11)
Arden School, Solihull

What Is Soft And Gentle?

Soft and gentle the blue sea shows
Soft and gentle the petals of a rose
Soft and gentle the feathers of a bird
Soft and gentle a woolly T-shirt.

Soft and gentle is like a baby's skin
Soft and gentle is a lion's chin
Soft and gentle the sand through my fingertips
Soft and gentle a guinea pig's lips.

Soft and gentle to me is that you share
Soft and gentle to me is that you care
Soft and gentle to me means calm
Soft and gentle to me means a fresh farm.

That is what I think soft and gentle is
Anything is soft and gentle but you have to imagine it.

Jyoti Pancholi (11)
Arden School, Solihull

Winter Leaf

Hanging on the twig of a tree,
Shaking forwards,
Backwards.
Any second it can fall,
On the pile below.
In the icy breeze,
The icy, chilling frost.
Fall gently, winter leaf,
Fall gently.

Oliver Jones (11)
Arden School, Solihull

Storm

Thunder sounds, hear the roar,
Lightning cries evermore,
See the rain crashing down,
Pounding on the peaceful town.

Then suddenly you see the sun,
Singing over the tuneless hum,
The thunder and lightning come to a stop,
The sun shines and I'm left in shock,

The shining sun leaves me in awe,
The Earth is left in Heaven's core,
The burning sun is the key,
To Heaven's hope, let darkness flee.

But nothing lasts I know for sure,
The sun can't shine for evermore,
The clouds will suffocate its light,
And end its final dying plight.

The sun is fading through the sky,
Heaven has made a holy lie,
The Devil is laughing, there are storms again,
The Earth is left in Hell's pain.

Chris Pickering (11)
Arden School, Solihull

Winter Leaves

Winter leaves
On the winter trees,
About to fall,
On the ice wall,
Winter leaves drift way
To the summer's break of day.

Tomas Griffiths (11)
Arden School, Solihull

Nature

Up in the tall, spider-webbed trees,
With the whistling breeze,
The branches are swaying,
And the squirrels are playing,
Oh the nature outside!

The hedges are tangled,
A bramble is mangled,
Some bees are collecting,
Their pollen for making,
Oh the nature outside!

Then a bang and a crash,
The lightning shall flash,
Some grumbling and a roar,
It isn't the same anymore,
Oh the nature outside!

Claire Fearon (11)
Arden School, Solihull

The Ocean's Roar

The light of day
The sun's ray
The ocean's roar
The whales snore.

The dolphins play
Throughout the day
While seagulls dip and dive.

This blueness is so great to see
This calm peace of my world
How wonderful it is to me
To see its greatness here.

Jamie Loftus (11)
Arden School, Solihull

Different Creature

Here on my balcony in New York
It's the rush hour so I hear the 'honk-honk'
I wish I could get away from here
I wish I could have something else to hear
Like the birds singing in the trees
The flowing river and the raging seas
The thought of lush, green grass
Instead of nuclear weapons and toxic gas
Or the trees blowing in the breeze
Or the whale's tail in deep, blue seas
Or the beautiful stars under a shining moon
Or even the splish of water on my head
Instead of families grieving over dead
New York is the dirty side of nature
How I wish I was a different creature.

Calum Frain (11)
Arden School, Solihull

The Outside World!

The sun is shining brightly,
Upon the summer flowers.
The rainbow that's in the sky,
After the spring showers.
The tall, green grass beside me,
Is tickling my feet.
A tree blown over in a storm,
Makes a wooden seat.
I look above the clouds,
And see the sun rise.
To see the nature all around,
I just open my eyes!

Rebecca Mendil (11)
Arden School, Solihull

As Autumn Begins

As autumn beings it starts to drive
Summer away like a lion chasing a deer.
Yesterday I took a walk in the woods to find some
Blackberries for my puds,
As I travelled I saw a hare, looked up and saw
The trees were almost bare.

Suddenly I felt a chilly breeze,
So cold that I began to sneeze,
The smells of earthy fields close by,
Make my senses come alive.
My eyes fell upon the blackberries,
Bristles on branches prickled my fingers,
Violet stains that still linger.

Now that the lion has caught its prey it has only to
Worry about the day
When the hunter appears . . .
Winter is coming.

Lutalo Lennox (11)
Bablake School, Coventry

Devil May Cry

The devils are always lurking around,
Around the dark and spooky places,
In horrible disgusting areas.

You can hear them through the floors,
Crying, crying and crying,
For someone to rescue their souls.

They're always trying to fight this evil,
That they lived in,
Waiting, waiting and waiting for forgiveness.

Daniel Lightfoot (13)
Bablake School, Coventry

June

As the young child's blond hair
Whistles past the wind,
As the sun burns down on
The young freckles of the skin,
And the food on the table attracting all the flies.

As the trees blossom
The leaves fall,
The spiders crawl around
Hovering and humming,

Boom!

A wasp as
The summer starts
And the winter fades,
As June reunites this
Long and lasting year.

Roseanne Louise Elkington (11)
Bablake School, Coventry

The Colour Black

Black is the tuxedo worn by men,
Black is the colour of ink in my pen.

A belt is black, as well as a leather shoe,
Little black buttons and the night sky too.

Black is like coal at the bottom of a sack,
The black hole in space is like a colossal Mac!

Black is dull, like a stormy night,
Black is a raven taking off for its flight.

Black is a Goth, not wearing decent colours,
Mostly black, not many others.

Black is smart! It never fools
Always to me, *black definitely rules!*

Abhimanyu Bose (12)
Bablake School, Coventry

Harley Davidson

For he is so sweet,
For he is so fun,
For he is my Harley Davidson.

When he is hungry,
He bounces in the garden,
Making it fun all around.

He likes to play all the time,
With a companion,
For Hannah is her name.

Every time he jumps,
Every time he lands,
Flump, flump, flump.

His cute, big eyes,
Look around and around,
Amazed from head to tail.

These are my reasons,
I love him so,
He is my Harley Davidson.

Caroline Peak (12)
Bablake School, Coventry

July

A beautiful woman they see it so,
In summertime her daisies glow,
Holding rays back from her face,
Watching children come and play,
Night-time comes and she is asleep,
The morning comes for all to see,
Blinded now but hears them all,
Have fun and play.

Mariam Ghadimzadeh (11)
Bablake School, Coventry

Attitude Food

I love food,
All sorts,
It puts me in a good mood.
I don't see why people,
Decide to eat trash,
That makes them dash,
Down to the surgery.
I love vegetables and fruit,
So I don't see why,
People give *them* the boot.

Apples, bananas,
Even cauliflowers,
They work like spanners,
Tightening up my energy.
People should always gobble,
Things that help them,
Not things to make them wobble.

So why don't *you* work,
To get rid of stuff,
That *doesn't* make you perk.

Harriet Carter (13)
Bablake School, Coventry

October Is An Aging Man

October is an aging man with grey hair
Sitting on a park bench with leaves blowing at his feet
He looks around and sees children playing with the leaves
He turns the other way and sees trees losing leaves fast
October is an aging man.

Jean-Paul Francis (12)
Bablake School, Coventry

Harvey

Day has come and all round the house not a creature is stirring
Oh, except Harvey!

A three-year-old puppy who loves to shout.
He'd bark at the door until I let him out.
He'd grab his rope and we would play tug of war.
He's going to win, of that I'm sure.

We'd have a wrestle, I'd go to ground.
Then outside he'd have a bound.
I'd go to the sofa and lie down.
He'd come skidding in and look at me with a frown.

When we went for a walk he'd drag me away.
But sadly he's not like this today.
Old and frail.
He still wags his tail.

When he hears me coming downstairs,
Very lovingly he stares,
With a wag of his tail and a twitch of his ear,
The sight of this old dog causes a tear.

Jack Lewis (12)
Bablake School, Coventry

The Joys Of Spring

Spring reminds me of babies when they are born.
It is a time when new buds appear on bare twigs and branches.
They grow into trees and bushes,
Making the countryside a beautiful place to be.

Babies are the same,
They develop so quickly after their birth.
The first smile, the first crawl, the first words.
They make everyone so happy
And put a 'spring' in everyone's step.

Michael Probert (11)
Bablake School, Coventry

The Elephant

The start of the day,
He wakes from a sharp hit.
What's on his back?
It's probably one of those humans.

They think they are the only importance of this world,
Especially that man that's bold.
He treats the elephant like a piece of dirt.
He even hangs chains around his neck.

The man contains him.
He is terrified of him.
Scared of attack, the elephants attack.
After all he is the strongest of them all.

Now you have heard the elephants say,
Help him,
Treat him well,
Because that's the end of his unpleasant day.

Chris Reynolds (12)
Bablake School, Coventry

The Ostriches

A car drives in and the engine cuts out.
Some creatures approach.
They look superciliously at the car.
The small head appears from the long neck.
The sharp beak bangs on the roof.
Bang, bang, the creature is attacking,
The sky blackens. The air is cold.
This creature looks very old.
It is an alien face.
The headlights are switched on,
And a bird is visible.
It is the dreaded, the nastiest . . .
The ostrich!

James Vallance (12)
Bablake School, Coventry

Horses

The horses snort, their breath turns to steam.
You can hear the angry stamping over the frozen field.
Their eyes blazing, their stare fixed.
Someone's entering their paddock.

The dark black horse lay with her precious colt,
Her daughter's grazing, unaware of the looming situation.
The gate squeaks as it opens.
A small pony in the distance is alarmed and breaks into a gallop.

The horses lift their heads at once.
Their tails have stopped swishing. Their ears are back.
They break into a canter.
Suddenly a blur of smooth colour goes flying past.

The horses approach the gate.
At first they do not realise.
But soon the fate will come.
They are going to be ridden . . .

Ryan Harmon (12)
Bablake School, Coventry

Spring

A little child with golden hair
Leaping around amongst the lambs
Snow-white is her frock
And pink are her cheeks
Like the spreading blossom on the trees.

Crocuses sprout at her command
Daffodils are swaying in the breeze
The trees will awake
From their lengthy sleep
All living things are alive again
Rejoicing in the sunshine and the breeze
Rustling the trees' living leaves.

Emma Gallagher (11)
Bablake School, Coventry

The Cat

Brown and black stripes are all you can see
When you are watching and looking at me.
I can be very lazy, lying around
But I prefer to be on the move.

Jumping and chasing low-flying birds
Pouncing on mice, that's also nice.
I want to be wild, I want to be free
Please, please, can't you free me?

I was taken away from mother at birth
I was stuck in a cage, is that all I am worth?
My brothers and sisters were taken as well
I want them to be right here, with me.

In my head I'm with every cat
The big ones, the small ones, the tigers, the kittens.
We are happy and free
And this is how we want to be.

Clare Jepson (12)
Bablake School, Coventry

October

An aging man wrinkled and down,
With a greying beard walks the town,
Dithering along and never,
Showing a smile whatever the weather.

He stands still watching the world's effects,
Whilst others around him share merry jests,
Jokes and Hallowe'en frights,
But still he stands through the cold nights.

Aaren Jon Healy (11)
Bablake School, Coventry

The Seasons

Spring, the season of newborn things,
Wonder how may creatures it will bring.
Lambs, calves, tadpoles, and many, many more,
Though what next spring will bring we cannot be sure.

Summer, the animals start to grow,
They begin to hunt by themselves,
For the days are longer and the nights shorter,
It gives them time to find their way home.

Autumn, the weeks will come and go,
With the trees swaying to and fro,
The leaves are falling down, down, down,
They make a gentle, rustling sound as they hit the ground.

Winter, a new time and age,
Everything is dull and grey,
No trees are swaying in the wind,
Just bare branches waiting to blossom.

Aisling Flanagan (11)
Bablake School, Coventry

January

A newborn baby, they see him as cute, light and adorable.
His bald head as smooth as snowflakes falling onto the floor.
His rosy cheeks glimmer as if there will be sun
But alas there is no hope for we're in winter.
We see him watching the children in the snow
And his eyes shine up but he is too young.
It is only January and soon he'll be out as well.
The winter's wicked wind blows,
The windows open as snowflakes trickle in and land on his nose and
Then we hear him chuckle.
It is then we know he is a winter baby.

Morgan Baker (11)
Bablake School, Coventry

October

October is like an old age pensioner,
The days are shorter and the sun moves slower,
The leaves on the trees are like the colour of hair,
Like gold, orange and red,
The cloudy skies make the old people grumble and moan,
The bare trees are like the old people's bones,
When they are all bent over,
The harvest in October is the memories,
And knowledge of old people,
Cold winter nights ahead.

John Masser (11)
Bablake School, Coventry

Chocolate

I love chocolate when it's melted,
Thick, slimy, gooey chocolate,
The way it drips off your spoon,
Forming a chocolate lake.

I love chocolate in a drink,
Hot with chewy marshmallows,
When you stir it with a spoon
It swirls into a tornado.

I love chocolate as a cake,
With tiny, little sprinkles,
The cream oozing off the spoon
Piled up in a high mountain.

I love chocolate as a bar,
With sweet raisins inside,
Caramel, toffee and nuts,
A whole landscape of sweetness.

Beth Hushon (12)
Bablake School, Coventry

Spring Sensations

Bare branches on the trees, blossom,
A baby brightens a parent's heart,
Plants, trees and flowers colour the land,
Children colour everyone's lives,
Sunshine beams over the land,
Smiles beam on young children's faces,
But spring can't last forever,
Neither can childhood,
The whole year and your life all
All evolve into a new chapter . . .

Hannah Mulhern (11)
Bablake School, Coventry

The Tortoise

Burrowing deep into the sand,
Sleeping silently, all through winter,
Popping back out of the hole he's dug,
To start the New Year.

Stretching slowly in the sun,
Crawling like a broken-down car,
Hungrily eating the food he's found,
Happy to be on the move again.

Showing off his patterned shell,
To the females prancing around,
Dozing in the long, green grass,
Not wishing for anything else.

Life for him is just beginning,
After all, he's only 60!

Rachel Ann Hollinrake (12)
Bablake School, Coventry

The Hunting Wolf

The stars of night shone down,
On the clear, forest floor.
Deserted, abandoned, nothing to see,
Not even leaves falling from the trees.

But a sound occurs in the forest gloom,
Like quiet thunder drawing close.
The insects flee as the noises increase,
And hidden animals cower in fear.

The wolf enters the scene,
His sleek and powerful grey body.
Running with the wind,
A nose seeking tonight's victim.

His teeth are waiting to be stained with blood,
As his paws hit the earth like bolts of lightning.
With a pack at his back he howls to the night,
While the earth trembles at the sight.

This powerful and stunning nightmare of the night,
Whose life is due to end.
With the crack of a gun his last hunt is done,
His carcass, a hunter's prize.

How many beasts like this creature,
Have fallen to sound of a gun?
How many more must die,
For man to be satisfied?

Rory Mark Doherty (12)
Bablake School, Coventry

The Shark

The great ocean twists and roars,
A trail of blood is left.
For those who travel alone,
Will face grave danger.

A young seal is struggling against the ocean,
And then it's gone.
Fishes fled when faced,
With this creature.

For the shark is deadly,
And shows no mercy.
For whom he meets,
In the deep, blue ocean.

His large, white teeth are waiting to be stained,
As he swiftly moves through the sea.
Quietly the shark moves to its prey,
Then it strikes.

The fish is twisting and struggling,
But it cannot escape.
Deeper and deeper the teeth go in,
Then the fish falls.

Tom Chen (12)
Bablake School, Coventry

The Snake

Slithering softly through the sand
Covering part of our land.
I love to see the different colours
Shimmering all around.

The snake shivers
Like someone frozen.
While the breezy air
Blows through my hair.

The creature approaches
About to strike.
It sticks out its long, thin tongue
And snips your skin.

Slimy skin, all slippery and cold
Is this what I will be like when I'm old?
In its cage it stays all day
Then when I come home we love to play.

It moves fairly fast
And all the memories will last.
As I watch the patterns of the snake
Slowly turning rough and jagged like a rake.

Slimy, slithery and smooth . . .
The snake.

Matt Black (12)
Bablake School, Coventry

The Pig

He lies sleeping in the sun,
Looking at the sky,
He wishes he could fly,
So do we.

He tramples over the newly-cut grass,
How he hates that smell,
It goes up his nose and out again,
There's a ringing; it's the bell.

He steals over to the food trough,
Eating merrily,
Suddenly a big man comes up to him,
And pats him on the back.

He feels warm now,
Nice and safe,
He's not in a mood now,
But it's too late.

There's an excruciatingly sharp pain,
Right in his neck,
He sees a bright light,
Alas, he's dead!

Abi Rewhorn (13)
Bablake School, Coventry

The Fly

Trapped in a hot, stuffy room,
Searching for a way out.
Throwing herself against cool, clear glass,
Staring desperately at the clear, blue sky.

Her delicate, silvery wings fluttering,
She flies around.
Her drone cutting through the humid air,
She explores her prison.

Furry antennae quivering,
Kaleidoscopic eyes looking for an escape route.
Legs scuttling across the window sill,
Leaving tiny footprints in the thick layers of dust.

In her last frantic effort to try and escape,
She flings her metallic blue body,
At the invisible barrier.
A failure. She drops to the floor.

Ami Shirley (12)
Bablake School, Coventry

The Spider

The glowing moon
Is out to shine,
Making the web glisten silver
Against the ebony night.

The thin, weak legs
Carry the black, bold body,
Circling and circling
As if it was a Ferris wheel.

As the night falls silent
He carries on working,
Silently spinning and spinning
Not a second to lose.

His body as black as the night,
His web as silver as the moon,
He's in charge of all creatures of the night
Known as the king of the Goths.

Nadine Minty (12)
Bablake School, Coventry

The Snake

It hides in its corner waiting to strike,
Finding the right moment to bite,
As the venom flows to the teeth,
A silence overcomes.

The heartbeat hardens,
As the snake prepares to strike,
Now it's time for the sleek snake's body to fly through the air,
Thud! He's stuck to the glass.

He slithers to his corner,
Spitting on the way,
His slimy tongue comes out and curls,
His familiar hiss in anger and fright.

Now he's tired,
Back in his corner,
There's no food coming for an hour or so,
So he hides in his corner waiting to strike.

Kenny Sangha (12)
Bablake School, Coventry

The African Elephant

The elephant stumbles across the deserted plain
Searching for water and longing for food.

His herd has died
And he is in despair.
What will happen to him?

The wait is over
He sees a lake.
He staggers towards it
But alas . . . a mirage, a fake.

He begins to tire
He is very weak.
The sun is beating down,
This is the end.

He lies down on the hot and dusty ground,
And makes no sound.

Once a huge, respected beast,
Now a lonely, worthless creature
Who was having trouble just to find some shelter.

Amandeep Mankoo (12)
Bablake School, Coventry

The Organ Grinder's Monkey

His little hat held pitifully out,
Begging the harsh passers-by,
To spare a shilling, a little change,
The organ grinder's monkey sat rejected.

No will to live left in his body,
An entertainment, not an animal,
His frail little body, weak and worn out,
Shivers in the autumn wind.

Tropical shores a distant, distraught memory,
No love from his master, just the crust,
Of a scrap of bread bought on a shilling,
As stale and cold as his master.

His jungle home ravaged by humans,
Family and friends packed into cages.
His freedom stripped from him,
In a show of utmost cruelty.

Old, cruel winter comes again to him,
Not fit enough to battle the cold,
Fighting a losing nightmare,
His pitiful body is buried in cold, hard ground.

Oliver George (12)
Bablake School, Coventry

Fun Through The Seasons

Spring, oh what a happy time,
Flowers bloom pink, red, lilac and lime,
People cheerful about newborn life.
Spring, oh what a wonderful time.

Summer, now she's a cheerful character,
A time of holidays, hot sunshine and laughter,
Children playing, oh what lovely sound
Oh how I can't wait for the season summer to come round.

Autumn, a time of colour,
Fiery red, orange and brown,
But soon the rain will come,
And knock them all down,
The weather gets cold, chillier as winter comes.

Winter, a cold, wet and dull time
As snow falls and all the plants die,
But there is another side to winter, making snowmen,
Snowball fights too, Christmas laughter and sticky puds.

These are the four seasons,
Full of fun,
Each and every one.

Emily Mason (12)
Bablake School, Coventry

Gerbils

As the sun rises, like a fiery ball
The group of gerbils wake up
And blink their eyes sleepily.

With fur as white as snow,
And small, glittering rubies for eyes,
They start to move in search of food.

They leap about faster than ever
Over the burning, sandy desert
Never resting, never stopping!

The sun starts to set,
They burrow together to rest
And sleep as the stars start to glitter . . .

And sparkle!

Vikki Jones (12)
Bablake School, Coventry

Life As A Year

The year is like a lifetime.
During spring, you are born,
Along with nature, plants and animals.
A fresh start.
Summer is like your 30s,
Everything blooming and bright,
Happiness around every corner.
Autumn is like your 70s,
Settling down, slowing down,
Putting the brakes on.
Finally, winter is like your death.
Everything dies, plants, trees,
Knowing that it will be back.
However, life isn't like that.
You only get one chance.
Remember that . . .

Ashleigh Lafaurie (11)
Bablake School, Coventry

Sonnet Of The Human Anatomy's Demise

A touch of red roses bleeds life once more,
In a yoke eternally burnt like coal,
Destroyed through the perforations of war,
Roses wilted, whilst death devoured our soul.

Beauty encompassed within Einstein's mind,
Shrank with the senile old man's dying day,
Nerves revealed what only my touch could find,
Rivers of light, a firework's display.

Sin stretched with vascular bundles exposed,
My metacarpals picked like a flower,
Twisting like twigs, within I was reposed,
Golden flames provoked, a scarlet shower.

Veins swell with quicksilver alive in hearts,
Plunging into death, I am struck by darts.

Selina Khan (15)
Beauchamp College, Oadby

Countryside In Winter

Winding rivers flowing through grassy banks
Elegant trees, tall and sturdy
Frost glittering on some fallen leaves
A cottage in the distance
Shining like a star
Warm, welcoming lights inside
A haven to the weary traveller
Light snow falling to the ground
Covering the now icy river
The cold, white moon
Lighting up the country lane
Horse and cart trundles along
Clip, clop, clip, clop
The sound of hooves
Echo in the night.

Elizabeth Ormston (11)
Bristnall Hall Technology College, Oldbury

Why?

All of my life I've wondered if there is anything more,
Beyond the world that I've lived in for so long,
What will happen to my body and soul? Nobody knows.

Are there such things as Heaven and Hell?
Or was Charles Darwin correct in saying there is no God?
Why do people die? What happens to them?

Is the Bible all it's made out to be?
Did God create the Earth?
Where will I go when I die?

Are ghosts and the afterlife real?
Will I come back to Earth as something else?
Or will I just die and that will be that?

These thoughts keep on going through my mind every day
Who am I? What am I? Why am I here?
I just don't know what to think.

Why do some people have disabilities?
Everyone deserves to live a normal life,
Don't they?

Why do some people have to suffer in pain and silence?
Surely no one should have to live like that,
Day after day, minute after minute, second after second.

Is there life on other planets? Do they know about me?
If there is what happens to them when they die?
Do they go to Heaven or Hell too?

What will the world be like in a thousand years?
Will there still be a world?
Who will live in it? What will it be?

Why?

Zoe Hunter (13)
Bristnall Hall Technology College, Oldbury

Wolves

Prowling through their dark domain
Confident in the fact
They are the horrendous hunters
The rest are their prey.

The strong, sleek body
The tense, tightened muscles
A spring coiled
Ready to be released.

Cloaked by the dank darkness
Not a sound is made
By their paws
Touching the ground.

They smell their prey
They get closer
The animal is unaware
Of their presence.

They pounce
A clamp of gigantic jaws
The wolves slink off into the night
A carcass is left on the ground.

Flesh hangs from their teeth
Their fur is matted by blood
The smell of death is on their coats
They go to kill once more.

Emma Hall (15)
Bristnall Hall Technology College, Oldbury

The First World War

I was hopeful to become a sergeant,
Just like my father had
I had just joined as
The First World War had begun,
We were by the trenches
When there was an explosion
Nearby,
I stood there, my legs as still
As steel.

Gas was overcrowding us,
So on our gas masks went.
Bill my cousin stood there,
Choking, spluttering, drowning
As the poison filled his lungs.

Then suddenly everyone started to run
And shout as loud as sirens and scream
When I noticed a bomb
Falling towards my father
I wanted to run forward
And grab him by the hand
Like I did when I was a young child
But
Too late, the bomb went off
I could feel tears rolling down my face like a river.

Why, why, why
Hadn't my father run away?
He should have seen it falling.

I lost my cousin and my father in this
Dreadful war.
Why did they have to die for their country?

Marie Evans (14)
Bristnall Hall Technology College, Oldbury

Please, My Young Children

Please, my young children,
This class is too loud,
I'll put you in detention,
There should be no sound.

Shut up, you old teacher,
I'll do what I want,
It's not my fault you're here,
Let me get on with my life.

Please, my young children,
This class is too noisy,
Stop talking, start working,
There should be no sound.

Shut up, you old teacher,
I'll do what I like,
There's nothing much to do here,
Let me get on with my life.

Please, my young children,
This class is too loud,
Stop whining, start listening,
There should be no sound.

Shut up, you old teacher,
I'll do what I like,
I'd rather be dead than do this work,
Let me get on with my life.

Suzi Jones (12)
Bristnall Hall Technology College, Oldbury

The Incredible Cow That Went To The Moon

Daisy was a clever cow,
Some things she does (don't ask me how)
Like reading, singing, even writing,
She even took up kung fu fighting!

But when she wanted to explore the moon,
'Space,' she said, 'I'll get there soon!'

She built a rocket straight away,
So she could go the following day.

Morning came, Daisy woke,
Ate her breakfast, drank her Coke,
Had a wash, used the loo,
And she was out at half-past two!

She packed some hot dogs and a tent,
But when she landed the rocket bent.
Daisy said she didn't care,
And for all I know she's still up there!

Megan Price (12)
Bristnall Hall Technology College, Oldbury

The Drunk

He hates his life,
He hates his town,
He drinks all day,
He's always down.

His time is up,
It's time to fly,
Back to his home,
Where he will die.

No one was there,
No one to hold,
For his life,
Was sad and cold.

Charlotte Nicholls (12)
Bristnall Hall Technology College, Oldbury

Winter

She is the cold-hearted queen of the season,
She is the chilling ice on the frozen leaves,
That lie on the slippery road.
She has the numbest face around,
And is the joker of the year.
She strips the trees with her long nails,
And bites and pinches whoever goes past.
She strangles the plants to their death,
Only the strong can survive.
She steals any happiness she can find,
And throws it away.
She is evil and sneaky,
She is the sharp end of an icicle,
Until spring comes.

Charlie Higgins (13)
Bristnall Hall Technology College, Oldbury

The Dark Eye

If you dare to look,
Be careful, do not stare,
For in his eye, is a private sky,
For he is the hair.
You see the black,
You see the pain,
You see his life,
The constant rain.
The people cry,
The blackbirds fly,
You see it in his eyes.
The pain goes on,
Through everyone,
And every day he cries.

Zoe Wood (12)
Bristnall Hall Technology College, Oldbury

Kill

In the morning so dry and bleak,
Lie the people fast asleep.
As the people wake the plague spreads,
Crawling around to get into their beds.

It snatches lives day by day,
People don't know it's coming their way.
As the days go by there are few people left,
Death is taking people by theft.

The plague is over,
In the docks of Dover.
Survivors rest in the houses in the bay,
Glad the plague has gone away.

People sob for loved ones' loss,
No comfort coming from the cross.
Funerals come in sixes or sevens,
The people float up into the heavens.

A year has gone by,
And the doves still fly.

Paige Boswell (12)
Bristnall Hall Technology College, Oldbury

War Poem

As I heard the enemies attacking,
We all ducked underneath the trenches,
As the bombs came flying over,
It was like a firework display.

The uniforms of our soldiers were wet and ripped,
Every minute there's a man dropping dead,
The soldiers that were dead were lying on the floor,
But every soldier that was alive wanted victory.

Our soldiers came with heroic optimism,
Now all they want is to win the First World War,
It was as if a trumpet was demanding attention,
With all different bombs flying over.

It was hard to tell what to do next,
As our sergeants were changing over from their duties,
It was like it had all ended when I finally got a rest,
But on my next duty it started all over again.

That's when I realised that by the end of the day,
I may not be alive.

Charlotte Cash (13)
Bristnall Hall Technology College, Oldbury

My Family Life!

I was born first, just Mum, Dad and me,
Just the three of us in our little family.

Whatever I needed they would come running,
Even though I was small I was incredibly cunning!

But all of a sudden it wasn't just me, Mum and Dad,
Home came a baby and things started to get bad!

His name is Jack my mum and dad said,
He is your little brother and he's having your bed!

They bought me a new one, it was big and bumpy,
I wanted my old one which was small and not lumpy.

I would shout, 'Mum!' and she would shout back,
'Hold on a minute, I'm dealing with Jack!'

It was my bed time so where was my Ted?
He was sitting over there in my little brother's bed!

When I came home from my nursery school
I saw something small that was starting to drool.

'It's your new baby sister, her name is Beth.'
'Oh no, not another new bed!' 'No, we're moving house instead!'

'Oh Mum, can we take her back and swap her for a Ted?
For you see I don't want a new house instead!'

Now I am older I wouldn't do without,
My little brother and sister even when they scream and shout!

Those two little droolers who stole my bed,
And borrowed my toys, even my Ted!

I love them to bits and am glad that they're mine,
And I wouldn't change a single step in time.

Holly Henderson (11)
Bristnall Hall Technology College, Oldbury

Fireworks

Vibrant sparks light up the night sky,
The colours burst from within.
Fireworks sprinkle the blackboard with glitter,
The Chinese dragon flashes like lightning.

They crackle until the morning,
Rockets belly-dance straight up to space.
The smiles appears on faces,
Fireworks represent happiness and grace.

Although they made a dazzle of light,
They slowly dissolve and disappear.
The sun has risen back up again,
And we wait for celebrations next year.

Sandeep Gahir (11)
Bristnall Hall Technology College, Oldbury

Dolphins

Suddenly they came, leaping through the waves
Gracefully they move
Water spills off their smooth, grey skin
Their eyes coming through the crystal water
As black as coal.

They're so daring and brave
Delicately diving into the waves
Happily and peacefully
They glisten through the water.

Wondering where to go next
As they glide through the ocean
As if they are flying.

Kate Jewkes (14)
Codsall Community High School, Wolverhampton

Not The Sun Or The Sea!

In the evening the soft, gentle moon,
Sits patiently waiting,
Romantically coming up every evening,
Watching over all the world,
Protecting us from the vigorous sea,
The glistening sparkle of silver catching birds' eyes,
The breathtaking view relaxing us every night,
No, it's not God or the sea, it's the moon,
Our good friend and it will always be!

Ryan Dil Sodhi
Codsall Community High School, Wolverhampton

Lamborghini Lover . . .

Its sleek, smooth body drags you in,
Taunting you, wanting you.
Its fierce face impatiently shouts,
And then its engine revs.
8,000, 9,000, 10,000 revs.
Its way of telling you come closer.
You go closer and everything is quiet,
Then you realise . . .
It's just a car.

Stephanie Evans (13)
Codsall Community High School, Wolverhampton

The Seas Of The Ocean

Cool . . . calm
The seas of the ocean
Waiting patiently
For that swift gust of wind
Gradually it takes its shape
A crystal-clear wall
Towering over itself
A shadow . . .
It rides on the wind for one moment . . .
Then crashes into clouds of foam
Dragging itself back, it's gone
No trace of what has just happened
It sits calmly again
Waiting . . .
    Patiently . . .

Hannah Kendall (13)
Codsall Community High School, Wolverhampton

There Goes Hollywood

A bird flies over,
Like a guardian spirit.
The misty hills, islands,
In the sea of fog.
It drowns thought,
Hate, love, and all
That would disturb peace.
It flows over the
Rolling landscape, purifying.
Dreams swirl in the mist,
Memories impaired, falling
Through the smothering white.
The mystical mists on mountains,
Bare, giving meaning to life,
Giving life to death.
His bony fingers reaching
Out to all wayward
Wanderers in the sea
Of life, money and beauty
Control populations.
Dreams of silver
Screen quotations take
Reality, feeling, love,
Good, compassion from a
World rife with torment.
And then 'cue the mists,
The rolling waves in the swirling masterpiece,
Islands floating.' and
'Exeunt impurities,
That's a wrap.'

Charlie Newport (15)
Derby Grammar School, Derby

The Camarauge Pony

As I stand stranded in the soaking field,
The rain trickling down my delicate cheeks,
I gaze around to see nothing but the stars shimmer on the ground.

Suddenly as I turn a sound locks into my ears,
A soft neigh was galloping towards me,
All that lived in me was fears.

A magical figure was coming at me,
I have discovered who the neigh belonged to,
A beautiful, gleaming white stallion stood there in the pitch-dark.

I tip-toed across the water-drained grass over to the horse,
I stretched out my weak, filthy hand to stroke the terrified pony,
The stallion and I had become great companions.

So that is the story of the camarauge pony,
He is now my greatest friend,
And we sail the heavens together.

Sophie Cohen (12)
Hillcrest School, Birmingham

The Lion

Scary lion on the street,
A scary lion I'll hate to meet.

A mane so hairy,
It looks like Jim Carrey.

Eyes so big,
It looks like it's doing a jig.

Teeth so sharp,
It could eat a koi carp and don't put your hand in it
'Cause it won't make you laugh!

A long tail,
It's as long as Abigail.

Scary lion on the street,
A scary lion I'll hate to meet!

Natalie Bruce (11)
Hillcrest School, Birmingham

After School

When the bell rings,
And I come out the door,
I think yes, yes, yes,
No more school!
I walk down the drive,
To the lollipop man,
The cars drive past,
I should have ran.
I walked down the road,
And into my house,
But I've got no homework,
It happened at last.
Out of my uniform,
And into my clothes,
On go my jeans but
Nothing on my toes.
Mom comes in,
I give her a hug,
So now she feels
Nice and snug.
When I've had my dinner,
And I'm watching TV,
My cat comes in,
And sits on me.
Later my sister,
Has started a riot,
Now I feel tired.
I brush my teeth,
And climb into bed,
When I open my eyes,
It all starts again.

Paris Sanders (11)
Hillcrest School, Birmingham

My Friend TV

When I come home after school,
I'm as bored as anyone could be.
I just sit and relax in front of the TV.
When I am tired and I'm lazy,
I watch TV.
When I sit with my family we have our tea.
We all watch TV.
It makes me laugh, it makes me cry.
My friend TV.

Mehak Tariq (11)
Hillcrest School, Birmingham

Baby Brother!

Smiling eyes,
Chubby cheeks,
Tiny nose,
Cute smile,
My brother.
Sometimes naughty,
Sometimes good,
He decides so don't you.
Every glance of him brings out the star,
I wish he was ten,
But he's only *four!*

Karina Binning (11)
Hillcrest School, Birmingham

My Life

I ran away that day,
Away from all the pain.
I have few words to say,
As pain will not wash away.

I thought dads were meant to love you,
To help you when things go wrong.
But my dad just hit me,
Try to make up with a song.

I couldn't take it anymore,
The bruises said it all.
When I fell to the floor,
I wrapped myself in a shawl.

Now I walk the streets of London,
With no family to care.
I'm miserable and desolate,
My mother's well aware.

Natalie Maclean (14) & Katie Elkins (13)
Kings Langley School, Kings Langley

Somewhere To Sleep

Homeless men, women,
And children, no place to sleep,
What a lonely world.

People walking past,
Stick up their nose like a mast,
I feel desolate.

I manipulate,
Only to make a living,
But what is the point?

Anna Mildner & Emma Parkinson (13)
Kings Langley School, Kings Langley

Dave

Bang! The door slammed,
Sleeping bag in my hands,
Ready for a life on the streets at 15,
Leaves rustling by my bare feet,
Skidding of cars across the streets,
Shouting and howling whilst the engines roared,
In London, Dave the tramp is my name,
No meaning whatsoever to passers-by,
With my hands cupped,` shivering with coldness,
Waiting for every penny to be dropped in my hands,
Hungry,
No one listening,
I am someone lost in the desert,
No one cares for me,
Dave, the tramp, that's all I am.

Adam Hurn (13)
Kings Langley School, Kings Langley

Nobody Cares

When you're homeless nobody cares
They give you dirty looks as they go by
They sneer spiteful comments like 'all you do is lie'
People poke you and prod you just because you're there.

When you live on the streets nobody cares
They look down at you as you are in disgrace
As if to say you have a hideous face
All your clothes have rips and tears.

When you sleep rough nobody cares!

April Clarke (13) & Jenny Brooks (14)
Kings Langley School, Kings Langley

The School Sonnet

Waking up for school is a dreadful drag,
I head to the bathroom and wash my face.
Finishing my breakfast I pack my bag,
Oh no! I'm late! I must pick up the pace.
I arrive at school at twenty to nine,
Before the bell begins to ring out loud.
In Geography we learn about the Rhine,
As the school students stand up tall and proud.
As the bell goes for lunch we rush outside,
We run down the stairs and speed to the courts.
We play football and happen to collide,
I go to matron and helped by all sorts.
As the Friday is ending I head home,
To end the Friday I am home alone!

James Witterick (14)
Kings Langley School, Kings Langley

My Life

My life is a planet far from the sun,
Desolate, empty, no light.
My life has no meaning; I want it to end,
To die, to be killed with no fight.

If there's any life at the end of the tunnel,
Then the tunnel has no end.
If someone can help me dig my way through,
I'll forever be their friend.

My life is a black and white film; there's no life
It's silent, lifeless and blank.
My well-spring of life is empty, bone dry,
All the opportunity's been drank.

Richard Allen (14)
Kings Langley School, Kings Langley

Fruit And Veg

The fruit and veg we eat are nothing like chips.
It's the horrible feeling whilst spitting out the pips.
Fruit and veg can't beat a good old sweet.
The smell of cabbage is like my feet!
The taste of onions makes me unwell.
How on earth do vegetables even sell?
Leafy cabbage that turns to sludge.
Cabbage can't beat a piece of fudge.
Chocolate and sweets in every shape.
You can't compare them to a horrible grape.
The sharp taste of a mango,
Can't beat a can of orange Tango.
The great taste of junk food
But fruit and veg will make you a dude!

**Warren Oakins, Christopher Malcolm
& Daniel Pischedda (14)**
Kings Langley School, Kings Langley

Fly Away Home!

I'm sad, I'm sick, I'm living rough,
Living on the streets is just too tough,
I was an alcoholic,
And that's just too symbolic,
Can't sleep, can't eat, can't get no love,
Too scared, too broke, just wanna choke,
And die, die, die,
Or fly, fly, fly
Away home,
Away home.

Naomi Elaine Sadiq & Lilli Swaffield (13)
Kings Langley School, Kings Langley

Holidays

Journeys are tedious and always drag,
The plane is infinite but has no space.
The food is plastic and the seats always sag.
Recycled air dries the skin on my face.
My room is tiny and not very clean,
From the window there is a boring view.
The pool is the smallest I've ever seen,
This would be better if I was with you!
The beach is quiet till the fight begins,
It's busy and frantic, I get no peace.
The ball lands in my drink, the kid just grins,
I wish I was at home instead of in Greece!
But the sun is hot, and I've got a tan,
Sorry! I'm staying, I've found a new man!

Iona Preston (14)
Kings Langley School, Kings Langley

Teenage Love

Lonesome all by herself night after night
Wondering and waiting. Where could he be?
Lusting for herself to be in his sight
This moronic affair has ended for her.
Not any admiration did she receive
Awkward conversation is what she gained.
All he seemed to do is hurt and deceive
In any circumstance he is the same.
Should she just turn around and walk away?
Can she keep letting him play with her mind?
Shall she be a fool and ring him to stay?
Her confidence has all been left behind
Yet she loves him always with all her heart
Though they are now eternally apart.

Grace King (14)
Kings Langley School, Kings Langley

Lizzie

Lizzie, the sadist in miniature form,
Teeth marks and rabies still indent my arms.
She walks round the house, bare as she was born,
My friends very soon are mentally harmed.
She pulls off ingenious stunts for fun,
I hide my head in shame as people stare.
Just watch as the scars and the damage done
Appear on the skin, go back if you dare.
I shield my ears as her voice pierces in,
A banshee let loose in my living room.
Expectations so high I just can't win,
'A pony, a castle', I face my doom.
Even though Lizzie is a dreadful girl.
She still means as much to me as does the world.

Caroline Hardingham (14) & Rebecca Davies (15)
Kings Langley School, Kings Langley

Sunday

What happened to the carefree day?
No car upon the road.
Why are the shops open?
Nobody needs to go.
What happened to the church
Filled with all its firm believers?
What about the family roast?
Now takeaways are eaten most.
What happened to our resting Sunday?
Why doesn't it exist anymore?

Ciara Parsons (13)
Langley High School, Oldbury

A Typical School Day

6.30am: *'Bbbrrr!'*
My eyelids slowly open.
I wonder where I am.
Then I suddenly remember,
It's Monday morning - *damn!*

I wish it were a Saturday,
I wish it were a Sunday.
Any day is better,
Than another school day.

I turn off the alarm clock,
And step out of bed.
I go down to the kitchen,
To make sure my tummy's fed!

Our dog Harry is sitting, staring at me,
I know he loves me the most.
I turn to get my drink and,
Harry nicks my toast!

I go into the bathroom,
To clean my teeth and face.
'Hurry up,' Mum shouts,
'Oh Mum, get off my case!'

I go back to my bedroom,
To put my school uniform on.
I pack my books into my bag,
'Oh no, where has Friday's homework gone?'

I say goodbye to my mom
As my friend knocks the door.
We slowly walk to the 128
Knowing school is beckoning once more.

We walk in through the school gates,
Dreading what the school day brings.
But then I see all my mates
And my spirits start to sing.

You know, school's not that bad,
Even the teachers can be quite cool.
The lessons aren't that boring
And the best things of all . . .

Are you and your mates, having a laugh
And having their support
'Cause any day can be great
When you and your mates have a great report.

Cherie Ellie Whyte (12)
Langley High School, Oldbury

The Pretty Perilous Perils
Of Primrose The Parrot

One day when her owner was in town,
Primrose the parrot,
Put on her dressing gown.

She flew across the living room,
She banged into the door,
Heaps and heaps of cloudy dust,
Blew across the floor.

She flew and fetched a battered broom,
She then started to sweep,
Eventually the broom gave way,
Primrose began to weep.

Her owner came back in from town,
She stared at all the mess,
Primrose sneezed the dust away,
It covered her owner's dress.

She flew to the dry cleaner's,
She flew over fields of mud,
She banged into a telegraph pole,
And landed with a *thud!*

Scott Bird (12)
Langley High School, Oldbury

Autumn And Winter

The cold wind arrives
As everyone sneezes
Our cheeks become red
By the autumnal breezes.

The weatherman says it will be very cold
As we get into December it starts to snow
The schools will close because of the cold.

We are near to Christmas
We buy our families presents
We see the nativity
And smell incense.

As we come closer to New Year's Eve
Our parents can't believe
How quickly the year's gone by
5, 4, 3, 2, 1, Happy New Year!

Adam Overton (14)
Langley High School, Oldbury

A Hungry Baby!

A baby cries in the night
Howling for food as it might,
It won't go to sleep
If it don't get to eat.

Held in its silk hands
A bottle comes to help,
The baby that cried soon drank the milk
Shut its eyes
And went to sleep.

The baby woke up
And cried at dawn,
'Be quiet, baby, or
I'll cook you an' all!'

Naomi Hughes (12)
Langley High School, Oldbury

Corrupt Child

Please, please just leave me alone
If you don't I'll run away from home
You've bruised my back with your leather belt
The way you hurt me is not the way to be dealt.

I'm only 7, I'm covered in cuts
Because my step-dad stubs out his cigarette butts
He picks me up by my sore arm
Throws me to the wall and acts all calm.

Last night my step-dad came in drunk
He sat right next to me and completely stunk
His hand started to slide up my leg
He didn't stop till I started to beg.

To this day I write this tale
Angry, sad and feeling betrayal
Locked up for life, I don't really care
He is to blame for all my despair.

Samantha Farrissey (14)
Langley High School, Oldbury

Do You Believe?

When I say I love you, do you believe it's true?
If you were to ever leave I don't know what I would do.
I can't live my life without you.
Do you believe that I will never lie?
Do you believe that I would love you until I die?
I would do nothing to hurt you and that is the truth.
If you don't believe me I will show you proof.
Now do you believe that I love you?
Well, if you don't, I promise you it's true.

Micha Grosha (13)
Langley High School, Oldbury

Who Are We?

Who are to say what goes?
Why do we complain?
Our life is better than many others
What's the point of all of this?

Who are we to say what goes?
People starve as we eat
And people thirst as we drink
What's the point of all of this?

Who are we to say what goes?
We have shelter while others freeze
And we have a bed while others cannot sleep.
What's the point of all of this?

Who are we to say what goes?
We are rich while others are poor
And we have what others need.
What's the point of all of this?

Who are we to say what goes?
We aim high and live a life
While others only dream
And we feel safe from harm
While others fear for their lives.

Who are we to say what goes?
We have warmth while others freeze
And who are we to say what goes?
We cannot even understand what really goes.

James Hewitt (14)
Langley High School, Oldbury

Distant Sounds

As I stand by the sea,
I stare into the distance,
I listen to the air,
It smells so sweet and rare.
What is that sound I hear?
Wailing sounds appear,
Distant sounds.
Is it the wailing sound of sailors,
Whose lives were lost in the wars?
The violent sea roars,
Distant sounds.
Violent waves thrash the shores,
Eroding ancient rocks,
It's funny, all these sounds,
Imagine what can they be?
Distant sounds.
I love the sea,
I love the air,
As I stop in a distant stare,
If I imagine what can they be
I could make the sounds speak to me,
Distant sounds.
These sounds I hear
Distant,
Magical,
Old and
New,
Stop and listen.
If you imagine hard enough,
These sounds could speak out to you!

Gemma White (12)
Langley High School, Oldbury

Why?

Why do I lie here in
My comfy, warm bed
    While they lie on the harsh
    Ground struggling for life?
Why do I sit here eating
As much as I want
    While they have never eaten in their
    Life as much as I eat in a week?
Why do I sit here
With everything I want
    While they dream of clean water
    And food?
How can I just waste
Money on sweets and clothes
    While they work for a few pence
    A day?
Why is it that I go to
Sleep knowing I'll awake
    While they take each day as
    A gift?

We are all the same,
But why are we different?
We all have the right to live,
So why do they have to live like this?

Lauren Waldron (12)
Langley High School, Oldbury

Tiger

Tiger, wild and free,
But so lonely.
Wondering forever,
Will you stop? Never.

Along the sandy trail,
You look so frail.
Inside however,
You're stronger than ever.

Tiger, strong and brave,
You will never crave.
No matter how far you run,
You will never be done.

There's fire in your heart,
It will never part.
Your life is a wonder,
It will be your plunder.

Tiger, wild and free,
How can it be?
You will soon die,
But your heart will still fly.
Forever.

Katie Louise Hillyer (14)
Langley High School, Oldbury

Christmas!

The air is crisp and filled with cheer,
Everyone's excited that Christmas is here!
Families have decorated their homes with care,
Tinsel is hanging from here and there.

Mistletoe is hung up in the hall,
The Cadbury's calendars are on the wall.
The gifts are hidden in Mom and Dad's room,
The house is not filled with an inch of gloom!

Carollers sing hymns for mince pies and sweets,
Christmas Eve we dream of presents and treats!
Cookies, milk and carrots we leave,
For Santa and the reindeers who we all believe.

On Christmas morning we jump out of bed,
At 6 o'clock like our mom and dad said.
The presents have been left under the tree,
We dash to see what we have with glee!

The family comes round to see what we've got,
We have Christmas dinner which we love a lot.
Everyone goes home late and off to bed we go,
Christmas Day was wonderful, ho, ho, ho!

Kerry Dalton (14)
Langley High School, Oldbury

She's Gone

Walking along hand in hand,
Thinking back to the old days,
Watching the waves splash onto the beach,
Into each other's eyes they did gaze.

They found a free bench,
So they decided to sit,
Snuggling up to each other,
When she had a fit.

She was shaking and couldn't breathe,
The poor man didn't know what to do,
He shouted for help till someone came running,
And they said, 'Ring an ambulance do.'

When the ambulance came,
The old man was distraught,
They wouldn't let him in the back,
But he fought and he fought.

When they arrived at the hospital,
He phoned his son John,
The doctor tapped his shoulder,
And said, 'I'm sorry, she's gone.'

Louise Thomson (12)
Langley High School, Oldbury

Doctor Jekyll And Mr Hyde

Dr Jekyll and Mr Hyde,
Who was on the evil side?
The Dr constantly wanting that drug.
A bottomless pit he had dug.
Then Mr Hyde, the murderous beast,
Focused his eyes on such a feast.
A little girl running down the street,
This little girl fell at his feet.
Instead of helping like a gentleman should,
He stamped his feet with a thud.
Into her back he stamped his leg,
'Please stop,' she started to beg.
Along came Enfield to save the day,
He said to Hyde, 'You're gonna pay.'
A sum was agreed, ninety pounds was fine,
Enfield told Hyde, 'You were not in line.'
The day after that they went to the shop,
Enfield thought the cheque was a flop.
Hyde, he banked it, the cheque was good,
However Hyde's eyes were filled with blood.
In the end Jekyll turned out to be Hyde,
So I guess they were both on the evil side.

Matthew Skeldon (14)
Langley High School, Oldbury

The Last Unicorn

She stands wild and untameable,
In the middle of the moon-drenched glade,
Her beautiful white coat glistening in the breeze,
Gracefully, she treads the ground with her cloven, silver hooves,
Her golden horn, sharper than any blade.

Her shimmering mane billows as she tosses her head,
Majestic in stature unlike anything else on Earth,
Her strong body gleams in the weak moonlight,
She stands alone, all her kind are dead.

She bends to drink from a sweet, still pool,
And stares at the mystical creature below,
Her reflection stares back,
And for a second she is no longer alone,
The illusion shatters - life is so cruel.

Glittering the colour of careless sea foam in the morning dawn,
The last unicorn stands proud,
Against the wavering beams of night,
In the shadow of the forest, though she may seem forlorn,
They will stare, unbelieving, at the last unicorn.

Francesca Joanne Holden (14)
Langley High School, Oldbury

Jungle Fever

There's no noise in the jungle,
Not a sound from the trees,
Not a sound to be heard,
From lions to the bees.

I could not hear a roar,
Or a tweet from a bird.
I just don't understand this,
Why no sound to be heard?

Not a single snake was hissing,
Not a single bear would growl.
Not even the brightest tiger,
Was going on the prowl.

Not a waterfall was going,
Not a single river flowing.
Why can't I hear a sound?
Are all the animals underground?

Not a crocodile was snapping,
Not a single parrot yapping.
I can't even hear the smallest fly,
Not even one flew into my eye.

I see a dam but see no beaver,
Everyone's caught jungle fever.

Benjamin Thomas Marshall (14)
Langley High School, Oldbury

Run Away

It was Christmas Eve,
I was just fed up,
I decided to leave,
Run away.

I packed my stuff,
Only the stuff I needed,
Like food and water and a blanket,
I opened the door and left.

It was pitch-black,
I couldn't see the path in front of me,
I couldn't, I wouldn't look back.
I ran.

I passed a house,
With an open window,
And what I saw,
Made me guilty.

It was a family,
Filled with joy,
Laughing and playing,
Like a family should.

This sight willed me,
I turned back,
And walked slowly,
To my home, to my family.

Matthew Hawkes (14)
Langley High School, Oldbury

Kids

Mini terrorists, that's what we are,
As we speed around the corner in the stolen car.
They're not like our generation they say,
That's what they say about kids today.

Just because we're all mischievous,
Doesn't mean to say our minds are devious.
They're not like our generation they say,
That's what they say about kids today.

Drinking, smoking and taking drugs,
Some people think we're thugs.
They're not like our generation they say,
That's what they say about kids today.

We are the scum of the Earth,
People wish our mothers hadn't given birth.
They're not like our generation they say,
That's what they say about kids today.

Alexandra Hoult (14)
Langley High School, Oldbury

The Best

This team dominates the beautiful game
Well known
You should know the name
They're the number one team
In the Hall of Fame.

Unbeaten for 49
Going for 50
If they do it
They'll make history.

Haven't lost to the rest
But it's Man U next
That'll be their toughest test.

If you haven't guessed it yet
Keep on guessing
'Cos I ain't telling
Nah, I'm only messing
It's easy
It's Arsenal FC.

Harinder Dhadda (14)
Langley High School, Oldbury

Nature

How small the lonely flower is,
Compared to the mighty tree.
How quiet nature's world has become,
Apart from the buzzing bee.

As the birds fly gracefully across the sky,
The brook continues to flow.
The fish swim, swim about freely,
And the grass continues to grow.

Out pops a little rabbit,
From his underground home.
He sniffs the air excitedly,
The fields are his to roam.

As the time has come, the sun does set,
And nature says goodnight.
Even cast in grey and black,
It's still the perfect sight.

Nichola Stephanie Thompson (14)
Langley High School, Oldbury

Hallowe'en

Hallowe'en, Hallowe'en,
Beware, take care,
You never know, you might be in for a scare,
People greeting, the children trick or treating,
Season's greetings everywhere,
Pumpkin heads with bright lights,
Scary costumes walking through the night,
Children's laughter,
As the witches cackle
The fireworks crackle,
While a woman hands out toffee apples,
The night is over,
At a blink of an eye,
For there were no children in sight.

Krizia Mills (14)
Langley High School, Oldbury

A Teenage Girl's First Crush

A teenage girl's first crush is . . . well, crushing.
Her body isn't hers, nor is her mind.
She finds herself shivering, shaking, blushing,
Weak, tormented, sick and going blind.
And why? Because some guy might look her way,
Then cast his eyes as quickly to the ground;
Some special one, for reasons she can't say,
Whose voice makes her feel faint when he's around.
But now my crush on you has been returned,
And so the two of us stand on some brink:
It can't be love so young, and yet we've learned
Love does its will, no matter what we think.
Slowly, slowly now - we mustn't rush:
Let's enjoy this first sweet teenage crush.

Hayley Cooper (15)
Pensnett School of Technology, Brierley Hill

I Love Food

I love to eat a jacket spud,
It warms me up and tastes so good,
It's nice with beans and grated cheese,
I always ask, 'Can I have another please?'

I love to eat chocolate cake,
Especially when it's one I make,
With chocolate drops and lots of cream,
I could eat it until my mom screams.

Pizza in a pan,
With lots of bacon and ham,
Mushrooms and cheese,
No anchovies please!
Tomato sauce and herbs on top,
Cut into slices, I'll scoff the lot!

Katie Winwood (15)
Pensnett School of Technology, Brierley Hill

Hallowe'en

Hallowe'en, Hallowe'en
The scariest time of the year.

All you ever hear is trick or treat
Just throw them on the floor and give them a beat.

You give them bags of sweets and money
But you still never see that sweet little bunny.

Big, round pumpkins stare you in the face
As you run around with gangs of mates.

Don't be afraid, don't be scared
Don't have a frown
Wear the Hallowe'en crown.

Devils, witches, vampires and more
It's all blood galore.

Becky Betts (14) & Natalie Fellows (15)
Pensnett School of Technology, Brierley Hill

I Love Pink

Pink, pink, I love pink
Bag, shoes, even ink
Any size, any shape
I even own pink tape.

Pink, pink, I love pink,
Is blue better? I don't think
Pink, pink everywhere
I even own a pink chair.

Pink, pink, I love pink
They think I'm daft 'cos I love pink
I don't care, I don't mind
'Cos pink's my favourite colour you'll always find.

Melissa McGregor (15)
Pensnett School of Technology, Brierley Hill

They Say

They say we can't be
Why do I want you with me?

They say we are too young
But we know our love will stay strong
You know me inside out
Why can't they see what our love's about?

They hate me to be with you
But I can't be without you
But love is weird
I've cried too many tears.

I love you I do
I hoped you'd love me too
We've grown apart and both made new starts.

I knew they'd win
I had to give in
I know I've lost you
But don't forget I'll always love you.

Aimee Garratt (14)
Pensnett School of Technology, Brierley Hill

Forgotten

There was a girl, her name was unknown
She went through her life all alone
Nobody to talk to or to help her through
And the dark, dull days of her childhood too
At least until the day they found her
But too late, she was gone, gone, gone
Only to be forgotten by everyone.

Zoe Nock (14)
Pensnett School of Technology, Brierley Hill

Windy Seasons

A gentle breeze for that warm, spring day,
Slowly trying to find its way.
Quietly trying to move around,
Ignoring the rubbish that's on the ground.

Summer's here, the wind is late,
Is it trying to hibernate?
Is it scared of the burning sun?
Or is it too tired today to come?

A stronger breeze for that autumn night,
Looking like it wants to fight.
Purposely disturbing all the trees,
Now most of them have lost their leaves.

As it gets to winter it becomes a gale,
Turning the children's faces pale.
Banging against the window and door,
Just waiting to fight a little bit more.

Will it be there when I wake up?
When I pour the tea into my cup.
Will it stay in bed for one more day?
Or follow me to school the very next day?

Stephanie Jones (14)
Pensnett School of Technology, Brierley Hill

Sausage

Sizzle, sizzle in our pan
Oh, dear sausage, you're our biggest fan.
Tasty, yummy, good looking too
Tomato, sausage we love you
Sausage and egg, sausage and beans
You cook so tasty in our George Forman grilling machine.

Kelly Morris & Jade Checketts (14)
Pensnett School of Technology, Brierley Hill

The Game

Life is a rugby game,
Friendship is a scrum;
People together,
Fighting as one.
When your team's got your back
You can go far,
Trying and scoring,
You are a star.

People grow apart,
And times they will change,
Familiar faces,
Soon become strange.
Standing alone,
Life is no fun,
You're holding the ball,
Better hope you can run.

Susan Marsh (15)
Pensnett School of Technology, Brierley Hill

The Staffordshire Bull Terrier

The Staffy is a dog
Better than all other dogs.
A little Staffy is a bundle of love
Whether it be black, brindle, pied or red.
They like nothing better than to lie on your bed.
The Staffy's bold and brave
But would never hurt a child
Not even in a rage.
The best thing about a Staffy
Is that they always make you happy.

Sam Cooper (11)
Pensnett School of Technology, Brierley Hill

Love And Life

At birth it is there before you
Your mother and father may have seen it too
When you start primary you see your first dove
But only in secondary do you think of love
When college ends you're in a flurry
The end of university, panic, you're in a hurry
You won't stop till you find the one you need
But till then must your heart continue to bleed
Then at last what you've been looking for
But much too fast you need it no more
From that day you decided to split
From person to person you start to flit
Once you realise you've found it again
Your heart loses recognition of such pain
The one you'll need and love for evermore
Will be there with you at Heaven's door.

Lucy Ashley (14)
Pensnett School of Technology, Brierley Hill

People Live In Poverty

A nice bubbly bath,
And a meal in a café,
For me it's a walk in the park,
But others are in the dark.

To ignore them is a disgrace,
For the whole human race,
People say it's a shame,
But life isn't a game.

Caring people raise money,
So others can buy food like honey,
Those who don't care are malicious,
I think they are vicious.

Jessica Bagley (14)
Pensnett School of Technology, Brierley Hill

Shopping

Shopping, shopping, I love you so.
Every Saturday I do go.
Trying on clothes and shoes.
So much to choose.
Shopping, shopping, I love you so.
When I have my money I go down Merry Hill.
Can't wait to have a credit card, run up the bill.
Shopping, shopping I love you so.
Shopping is so splendid.
Been wasting my money since I was a kid.
Shopping, shopping, I love you so.
Lots of make-up I love to buy.
In Boots I always try.
Shopping, shopping I love you so.
I love Christmas when it's the sales.
Then go outside to the wind and gales.
Shopping, shopping I love you so.

Samantha Williams (14)
Pensnett School of Technology, Brierley Hill

Up The Villa

I stand in the halt end,
We all jump up to sing,
As we watched Vassall take the bend,
Then he scored and we all said, 'King.'

Sorenson saved the goal,
We just scored 2-0, up the Villa,
Too bad for Ashley Cole,
It's a shame for Kenny Miller.

We just started to sing,
When will it end?
What's this thing?
They scored, we didn't defend.

Richard Marshall (11)
Pensnett School of Technology, Brierley Hill

My Mom

My mom is the best
Better than the rest.

She is a very good cook
But doesn't need a cookbook.

But when she is out
She'll never flout about.

My mom has a mate
Who we think is great.

She has big, brown eyes
And eats lots of pork pies.

We'd like to say thanks
As we lead her a dance
Our Stu, our Shaun, and me.

I love you, Mom
Because you're the great one.

Aimée Tibbetts (11)
Pensnett School of Technology, Brierley Hill

Football

Blow the whistle, kick it off,
Pass it back, go in tough,
Turn around, pass about,
Man on, give him a shout.

Dirty challenge, come on, ref,
Calm down, lads, it's not like death,
Down the wing, cross it in,
Volley it, there's your din.

One nil, two nil, three nil, four,
Hit it hard, along the floor,
Penalty claim, that dive was lame,
Get up and get on with the game.

Shane Bennett (12)
Pensnett School of Technology, Brierley Hill

Friday Night

Skating down the hill
Going very fast,
But if I fall off
I'll need a plaster cast.
Playing on my PlayStation
Lying in my bed,
Because I fell off
And bumped my head.
Playing on my keyboard
Making up a tune,
Mom comes up the stairs
With ice cream and a big spoon.
Picking up my book
Read a little rhyme,
Got to finish this poem
It's nearly my bed time.
Turn off my light
Get into bed,
It's the end of my day
Oh, I've just realised tomorrow's Saturday.

Stevie Davies (11)
Pensnett School of Technology, Brierley Hill

Cricket Match!

Eleven players on one team
Whack the ball, shout and scream!

Catch the ball in your hand
Don't let the ball decide to land.

Hit three stumps to get 'em out
You'll always win, never doubt.

One hundred runs, maybe more
Glide and slide gently to the floor!

Suman Chauhan (12)
Pensnett School of Technology, Brierley Hill

Music 'N' Dance

M is for Madness, with Baggy Trousers,
U is for U2, who are having a Beautiful Day
S is for Steps, who have a big Tragedy,
I is for Ian van Dahl, who thinks he's building Castles In
   The Sky,
C is for Celine Dion, who thinks everybody's Heart Will Go On,
N is for Norah Jones, who is Waiting For The Sunrise,

D is for Darkness, who have a feeling of Believing In Love,
A is for Abba, who think they are the Dancing Queen,
N is for Nelly Furtado, who thinks she's Like A Bird,
C is for Coldplay, who are imagining everything is Yellow,
E is for Elton John, who is asking everybody if they're
   Ready For Love.

Liam Guest (12)
Pensnett School of Technology, Brierley Hill

Ode To Merry Hill

My favourite place is Merry Hill,
My dad doesn't like it because of the bill.
If I don't have new shoes,
I always get the blues.
The clothes are very cool,
But the prices are very cruel.
Really nice tops,
Are in lots of shops.
Claire's Accessories is a girly shop,
Go in JJB's for a football top,
Plenty of places to eat and drink,
Some other places to sit and think.
Up and down people ride,
Steps that move and lifts that glide.

   That now ends my journey round Merry Hill.
   I'm now going to join the queue and pay at the till.

Zoë Westwood (11)
Pensnett School of Technology, Brierley Hill

Buffy And Bertie

You may just be a rat and a dog,
But you're still better than a cat and a frog.
I love to take you both for a walk,
Even though to you I can't talk.

You may not be exceedingly smart,
Though you're both still as fast as a dart.
And when I go and get a biscuit,
You look at me as though you want to nick it.

When you sleep you look cute,
But you never could be a mute.
I love it when you lie on my tummy,
Because you both look so funny.

Buffy and Bertie, you look so sweet,
I'm very surprised you both like meat.
I hate it when you look sad,
Because it makes me feel really bad.

I could cuddle you both every day,
I love you both in every way.
You both look cute even when you're sick,
For *best pets in the world*, you deserve a tick.

Sian Compton (11)
Pensnett School of Technology, Brierley Hill

My Dog Simba

You stare at me with your big, brown eyes.
When you try to catch those flies.
You look longingly at my dinner plate.
Like you've just made a great new mate.
I love to take you for a walk.
With my cousins we all talk.
You love me to tickle your tum.
So much you wiggle your bum.

Stacie Boswell (11)
Pensnett School of Technology, Brierley Hill

Does He Love Me Back?

I tell him I love him every day,
He looks at me and says ok,
I say to myself is he being true to me?
Is this relationship meant to be?
Does he love me back?

I see him hanging round with his mates,
Talking about their first dates,
Thinking they're special, something else,
Then on a night I sit there alone in my house.
Does he love me back?

I only see him sometimes,
Break times,
He doesn't realise I love him more than ever,
Until the end of my tether.
Does he love me back?

Jade Field (12)
Pensnett School of Technology, Brierley Hill

Dancing!

Dancing, dancing
1, 2, 3
Dancing, dancing
Swing to the beat
Dancing, dancing
Move your feet!

Dancing, dancing
All day long
Dancing, dancing
To a song
Dancing, dancing
1, 2, 3
Come on, come dance
With me!

Rebekah Gallimore (11)
Pensnett School of Technology, Brierley Hill

Why Me?

I get kicked, shoved
Punched not loved
I get stuffed in a bag
Burnt with a fag.

Is this love?
I cry at night
I hold on tight
Why me? Why me?

I got dumped in a gutter
I got stabbed with a pen
Attacked by a hen
Why me? Why me?

I got thrown in the river
I got stuck with a permanent dither
I got my ear ripped off by a swan
Why me? Why me?

Now I'm sitting on a cloud
Looking down
Thinking, *I'm gonna get you now.*

Alexandra Shevlin (12)
Pensnett School of Technology, Brierley Hill

Boys

Boys think they know it all
They think that they're the best
Boys think they're good at football
But they don't know how to dress.

Boys think they know the answers
To the test they haven't had
Boys act big and strong
And I hate it when they act bad!

Charlie Joanna Craig (11)
Pensnett School of Technology, Brierley Hill

Clowns!

Clowns are funny,
They make you laugh.
They make you happy,
When you're sad.

They wear coloured wigs,
And do silly jigs.
They wear baggy clothes,
And a big red nose.

They lift your spirits high,
So you'll never cry.
They have lots and lots of jokes,
For the nice old folks.

Clowns are funny,
They make you laugh.
They make you happy,
When you're sad.

Emma Dalloway (11)
Pensnett School of Technology, Brierley Hill

My Family

I have a mom who cleans the dishes
And tells us to say pardon.

I have a dad who feeds the fishes
And does all the garden.

I have a sister who's like a blister
Sticking out my skin.

And me, I'm just perfect
On the outside and the in.

Paige Grosvenor (11)
Pensnett School of Technology, Brierley Hill

Best Mates

We're mates that are the best
Together we live in the west.

Aimee, Paige, Chloe, Laura and Lisa
At our sleepovers we enjoy a pepperoni pizza.

Little sisters are a pest
They always give our patience a test.

Boys think we're little brats
We think they're like smelly, horrible rats.

Chloe fancies the older boys
But always ends up with toy boys.

Lisa is really thin
She is as thin as a pin.

Paige is always singing a song
She annoys us loads 'cause she wants us to sing along.

Laura is always shopping
At every shop she is stopping.

Aimee is a neat writer
And a good fighter.

We are best mates that have a good time
We will never commit a serious crime.

Laura-Jade Morgan (11)
Pensnett School of Technology, Brierley Hill

Dancing

Dancing is my favourite hobby,
It lifts my mood and makes me jolly.

When the music starts and I hear the beat,
I find it hard to control my feet.

The faster I move the more I swing,
I imagine myself like a bird on the wing.

Lisa Marie Rowley (12)
Pensnett School of Technology, Brierley Hill

Manchester United FC

The Devils go marching into Old Trafford fearless of any team,
Will we win or will we lose?
If we lose the crowd will be cheerless.
The crowd is roaring at the moment,
Let's make their spirits even higher.
Man U are off to a flier,
1-nil, 2-nil, 3-nil, the goals are flying in by Man U,
The crowd are off their feet, jumping off their feet.
Half time, Rooney 2, Giggs 1, 3-0 Manu U.
Second half Rooney scores a fabulous free-kick,
Rooney hopes Beckham was watching that,
With a smile, with a tick.
Fenerbahce scores 2 in a matter of 3 minutes,
While people were buying tickets.
Man U score another 2. What's the score?
6-2 to the Devils, we win.
The whistle blows, the match is finished.
Man U go in the changing rooms winning great,
In the Premiership and the Champions League!

Callum Giles (11)
Pensnett School of Technology, Brierley Hill

Food!

Food is good, food is yum,
It goes down in your tum, tum, tum!

Food is great, food is nice,
Food like chocolate tastes twice as nice!

Food is nice, food is great,
Sometimes you have it on a plate!

If food was a test I'd give it a tick,
Lots of food can make you sick!

Amy Sankey (11)
Pensnett School of Technology, Brierley Hill

Tigger

Orange and black mean stripes for Tigger
He bounces all day like a figure
He's nice and cuddly like Pooh
Do you like him? Because we do.

Tigger and Pooh went around the corner
And found a baby at California
They ran around all day
But all they seem to do is want to play.

They all watch him every day
Until they go and play
Winnie the Pooh and Tigger too
Hang around with Kangaroo.

Tigger is good, Tigger is fine
Sorry to say Tigger is mine
Tigger is the best
But he is also a pest.

Sarah Smallwood & Mary Hall (12)
Pensnett School of Technology, Brierley Hill

Pinky And Perky

Once I had some goldfish
I won them at the fair
They died a few months later
It left me in despair.

I thought my life was over
Like I'd fallen down the stairs
Once I had some goldfish
And they were like a pair.

Gemma Louise Bolton (11)
Pensnett School of Technology, Brierley Hill

Bullying Poem

1 pound, 2 pound, 3 pound, 4, he's got my money,
Why does he want more?
5 pound, 6 pound and now it's 7, 8 pound
9 pound, 10 pound and 11.

They took my shoes and my Rolex
I asked, 'Dear Lord, what's going to happen next?'
They took my new tie and they took my coat
They picked it up and put it in the pool
And watched it float.

I come to school, it's always the same
Picked on by bullies with no brain
On Tuesday it gets really hard
And by Friday I'm truly sad.

I went into the classroom
He looked into my eyes.

Ali Tahir (12)
Pensnett School of Technology, Brierley Hill

School

School is fun, school is cool
So come on and don't be a fool
Pensnett School is the best
Pensnett is better than the rest.

Lessons are good and the cooking's nice
In the kitchen you won't find any mice
So come to school, don't take the day off
Even if you've got a really bad cough.

Kerry Roper (11)
Pensnett School of Technology, Brierley Hill

It's A Fishing Trip To Remember

It was a fishing trip to remember
I caught a fish on an apple
I never seen it before
As I eat around my apple core
My rod twitched
As I itched
It was too slow
I felt so low
I wanted my dinner
As my belly was getting thinner
I lost my comb
I wanted to go home
I felt cold
My dad came
I felt the shame
I was on my way home
I found my comb
We unpacked
My dad was sacked
It's a fishing trip to remember.

Daniel Mallen (12)
Pensnett School of Technology, Brierley Hill

TV

If you don't like TV
Listen to my rap and you will see
Don't keep goin' to the loo
Just keep watchin' BBC2.

If you don't like raps you will see
Mine is sweeter than tea.

Some raps are fast
Some raps are slow
You hear more raps
Than Homer says, 'Doh!'

Aaron Moore (11)
Pensnett School of Technology, Brierley Hill

Seasons Change

Winter is coming, getting very cold
Put your hat and gloves on or you will be froze.

The leaves are crunching under my feet
As I'm walking down the street.

The wind is whistling in my ears
Makes my eyes full of tears.

Chestnuts falling off the trees
As bonfire night slowly appears.

Fireworks lighting up the sky
Pretty lights catch my eye.

Snowflakes falling on the ground
As I walk it makes a sound.

Christmas is here, presents all around
The joy of Christmas music, it's a beautiful sound.

Kayleigh Woodall (11)
Pensnett School of Technology, Brierley Hill

Dance Music

D isco dollies
A nd
N utty nannies
C rowded round the dance floor
E veryone dancing all night long

M usic and dance are what I like best
U p beat tempo
S o much better than the rest
 I n the disco it's so neat
C ome on, feel the beat.

Chloe Jade Wood (11)
Pensnett School of Technology, Brierley Hill

Darkness

She is doomed to walk the earth alone,
Her presence there but not known,
She takes upon the shapes of items,
That is until the dreadful light comes.

She cries in her background, no one cares,
She is known to no one,
Only mentioned in nightmares.

She yells at the top of her lungs,
But she stays silent, voice not strong,
She'll sit in a corner beside a chair,
She witnesses nothing but can't help to stare.

She is frightened when she hears the chime,
She weeps and weeps as she knows it's her time,
And then comes the light, rests the blanket and laid,
The poor girl has no choice but to wipe her tear and fade.

Mathew Parkes (14)
Pensnett School of Technology, Brierley Hill

Love

It makes you happy, sometimes sad,
Can feel very good or extremely bad.
When you have it, you can't help but smile,
Even if you feel it for a little while.

What am I talking about you might ask?
It's one of the world's hardest tasks.
It's resembled by a white, peaceful dove,
So there's only one thing it could be
And that is love.

Jade Nixon (11)
Pensnett School of Technology, Brierley Hill

I Wish I Could Rule The School!

Here I am snoring away,
I am here every day,
Snoozing and cruising, paying no attention,
It could be better in detention.

If I was headmaster of the school,
I would fire a teacher for breaking the rules,
If I did PE the teachers would be in the cold,
'Hurry up, run faster, you are much too old.'

If I did History and they messed about,
It would be no mystery, 'Detention!' I should shout,
If I did English and a boy was chewing,
Or had done something wrong,
I'd get him out and make him sing a song.

If I did Maths and a gang of girls were putting on make-up,
I'd get them out of their seats,
And have a look at all of the rude words
That they had put on the blackboard,
And they would say, 'Sorry, Miss, you are the lord.'

So here I am snoozing and cruising away
When I could be running the school all day.

Mica Williams (12)
Pensnett School of Technology, Brierley Hill

Safety

S is for safety that is important in the lab.
A is for accidents you should not have.
F is for fun if you do things safely.
E is for everyone doing things in safety.
T is for tidiness that is good to you.
Y is for your safety in everything you do.

Gemma Bradley (11)
Pensnett School of Technology, Brierley Hill

See It In A Boy's Eyes

He walks past me every day
Without a glance or a smile
I wish he would look my way
Or just talk to me for a while.

He talks to other girls
They giggle and they touch
Flashing their fancy pearls
I can't handle it, it's just too much.

I sit behind him in class
Wanting him to turn to me
I stop the girls who try to harass
But he still seems to see through me.

I walk up to him in the playground
I'm tired of playing his game
I told him I wait for him to turn around
And that I really like him and hope he felt the same.

He laughs in my face
But I still love him dearly
It's like we're in a special place
When he told me he loved me really.

Sarena Sharma (13) & Keisha Cramer (12)
Pensnett School of Technology, Brierley Hill

Animals

A nts get eaten, trodden on and not cared about.
N ever would that dolphin get pulled into shore by a knife.
 I n Britain fox hunting is legal when I think it should be banned.
M ore animals in the world are becoming extinct.
A nimals such as whales are killed for their oil.
L ove animals in every way.
S eals are being beaten to death by a baseball bat.

Mikayla Danks (11)
Pensnett School of Technology, Brierley Hill

Playtime

Fed up with school,
Can't wait till break,
All these lessons,
I can't take.

I wish it were playtime,
Can't stand it in here,
I'd rather be outside,
Where I laugh and cheer.

So please, teachers,
Let us out,
Let us have break,
Where we will shout.

The bell has gone,
It's time to go out,
Now it is playtime,
Where we run about.

Rebecca Gordon (12)
Pensnett School of Technology, Brierley Hill

Boxing

Mike Tyson is the best
He can fight
He gets in the ring
Then fight, fight, fight!
He punches his opponent
And he goes down
The ref counts 1, 2, 3
He has won!

Aaron Dunn (11)
Pensnett School of Technology, Brierley Hill

Chocolate Rhyme

Chocolate, chocolate, chocolate
It's all I ever eat
Every day of the week
This luscious, creamy sweet!

Chocolate, chocolate, chocolate
Smooth, dark, rich
This food I will never ditch
But when I eat too much I always get a stitch!

Chocolate, chocolate, chocolate
Milky, dark, white
Always in my sight
Every day, every night!

Chocolate, chocolate, chocolate
I eat it any time
Even with goo or slime
That's why I made a chocolate rhyme!

Stacey Hillman & Sonia Lal (13)
Pensnett School of Technology, Brierley Hill

War

War is a cold-hearted, monstrously wrong thing!
All the pain, all the fear and death.
Broken hearts and broken families.
When war is declared nations go in
And a full injured village comes out.

Death is creeping, creeping, creeping.
War is killing, killing, killing.
Anger and sadness is growing, growing, growing.
War is wrong, wrong, wrong, wrong!

Richard Hooson (11)
Pensnett School of Technology, Brierley Hill

PlayStation Fame, Brilliant Game

Run, jump, shoot, duck
Oh, that baddie's got a knife
This is skill not luck
Time to grab that extra life.

Here come the baddies
Clothes ripped like the Incredible Hulk
He spits when he talks
He'll shoot anything that walks.

Play the game
Win for fame
Lose for shame.

Oh no, it's s a glitch
This game's a real bitch
Turn left, turn right
The end looms, the goal is in sight.

Dwayne Grice (13)
Pensnett School of Technology, Brierley Hill

Heaven Or Hell?

Family is important, they're better than money.
They twinkle and glisten, they glow in the dark.
They'll go straight to Heaven because they are loving and tender.

But the people who have killed Russian children
They'll go straight to Hell
Because they're bad and mean
They're Heaven's enemy!

Nancy Lauren Howell (11)
Pensnett School of Technology, Brierley Hill

Life At Pensnett!

B ullying happens a lot to us!
E verybody in English is noisy!
C helsea and Becky meet in yr 7!
K icking and punching goes on a lot!
Y r 7 is worse than yr 8!

A nybody can be something!
N ever lie 'cos you always get caught out!
D ays go by as I do my work quickly!

C are for others and they'll care for you!
H iha Tahir is one of our best mates!
E veryone gets treated as one!
L evels matter to your future!
S ay hello every morning!
E verybody knows each other!
A nybody can become one!

And
  that's
    the
      end
       of
        my
         poem.

Rebecca Perkins & Chelsea Dunsmore (13)
Pensnett School of Technology, Brierley Hill

War

You watch it on the news
You hear people talking about it
But they will never really know what happens in the real world
Every day another hostage or soldier dies
Families make the hurting stop by saying it's lies, lies, lies.

Emma Hughes (11)
Pensnett School of Technology, Brierley Hill

Football Poem

Football is the game I love
I go and watch my local team
Even though our goalie only has one glove
My team comes out full of beam.

Half time comes, we are drawing 0-0
Our white shirts are ripped
'Let's get back out there and win,' says Phil
We got the ball and with the ball he kicked

Goal!

End of the match came, we won!
I can't believe it, we had moved up a place!
We had some fun!
I thought we would lose because one of our players tripped over
                                                            his lace.

Louise Williams (13)
Pensnett School of Technology, Brierley Hill

My Mom

My mom is cool, my mom is sweet.
I have to keep my bedroom neat.
She has a lot of patience but occasionally she shouts.
I know sometimes I deserve a clout.
I love her, I love her, I really do.
Remember your mom's always there for you.
When I'm sad or feeling down.
She'll say let's go shopping round the town.
My mom and my dad put up with so much.
But then never lose their loving touch.
When I'm feeling poorly or in a lot of pain
Mom's always there for me again and again.

Kimberley Mansell (11)
Pensnett School of Technology, Brierley Hill

My Brother

My brother had a cover,
He's name was Dilly Dover,
He went to the shop,
And bought a big chip.

My brother had a cat,
With a very big hat,
He sat on the loo,
And had a little poo.

My brother had a golf club,
And carries it to the pub,
He got very drunk,
And called someone a punk.

My brother got a beating,
While he was eating,
He fell to the floor,
And got up for more.

They rushed him to surgery,
With a big, massive Budgerie,
He didn't have a clue,
And kept saying moo.

Rebecca Newby (14)
Pensnett School of Technology, Brierley Hill

Sleepyhead

Climb the wooden hills
My sleepyhead
Now it's time for bed
Let daylight dreams fade away
For tomorrow is another day
Hurry off to bed
The sandman is coming
So rest your head!

Sara Allen (12)
Pensnett School of Technology, Brierley Hill

I Love The Way . . .

I love the way you look at me and smile,
I love the way you look and stare,
I love the way you look at me,
But if only I knew,
But I love the way you think,
I love the way you look,
I hate the way you left me,
But that's the way I took,
If only I had sense,
I didn't deserve what I got,
If only I knew where you were,
We could make it better,
But for now I talk to someone else,
And say you're just a friend,
Just in my mind,
The love of my life,
Forever again.

Kirstie Bavington (12)
Pensnett School of Technology, Brierley Hill

School

School is a prison,
Which holds us within.
Every teacher is an Anne Robinson.
Even the sound of a pin,
Makes us cringe.
The teachers are slave drivers,
Who make us whinge.
We are the screw while the teachers are the screwdrivers.

Thomas Savary (13)
Pensnett School of Technology, Brierley Hill

Suicide Note

Whispers, voices, mutters,
They all creep around in my head,
My alarm clock screams at me,
As I turn in my bed.
It starts again,
My depression rises,
As I try to live with people,
But they are all in disguises.

I sit here in my room,
Tears flowing out from my eyes,
And blood from my veins,
I've done it again,
But this time I shall succeed.
I am lying in my own pool of blood,
Please, Mum, do not cry,
I am happy now,
I wanted to die.

Love you forever,
Claire X

Claire Hunter (13)
Pensnett School of Technology, Brierley Hill

She's Gone

I cheated on her, I know it's wrong,
But I've been with her really long,
She did bore me towards the end,
But she was my bestest friend.

But now she's gone,
We've both moved on,
There's nothing I can do,
That's it, the end, we're through.

Yasmin Field (13)
Pensnett School of Technology, Brierley Hill

Autumn

Autumn is the best time of year,
In the trees you can see a misty deer.
Squirrels play in the trees,
Where they play in the frosty leaves.

Autumn is here,
It's that time of year.
Brown and red robins,
Look out for the goblins.

Conkers on the trees,
Makes me want to sneeze.
The sun is so bright,
I have a good sleep at night.

Lisa Bradley (12)
Pensnett School of Technology, Brierley Hill

Autumn!

All the leaves are on the floor,
Brown, orange, yellow.
On the trees,
There are no leaves.
Conkers on the ground,
It's dark at 8pm
And the boys and girls go to sleep.
At night the frost comes out,
He freezes the whole park,
And it's cold in the dark.
The children wake up,
As cold as they are,
And it's another chilly, autumn day!

Brett Welding (12)
Pensnett School of Technology, Brierley Hill

Sad Angels

Beaming in the sky
As a lighted candle in the window
No one knows how life can be
Shining through as if it was me
Close by I heard a voice
As gentle as a fly
Shimmering down as bright as a candle can be
A tear dropped from my face
It was an angel in disguise
I smiled in a glimpse
And in her deep blue eyes
I saw the sadness
And she sadly disappeared
In a beam of light
But I still remember her deep blue eyes.

Hina Tahir (13)
Pensnett School of Technology, Brierley Hill

Mates

Mates are good
Mates are cool
They never leave you
They come with you
Mates are good
Mates are cool
If you are unhappy
They comfort you
Mates are good
Mates are cool
They ask you round
Day in, day out
Mates are good
Mates are cool
That's what mates are there for.

Jodie Wood (12)
Pensnett School of Technology, Brierley Hill

Forever Autumn

The summer sun is fading
As the year grows old,
Darker days are drawing near.
The winter wind will be much colder,
Now you're not here.
I watch the birds fly south,
Across the autumn sky.
One by one they disappear.
I wish that I was flying with them,
Now you're not here.

Like the sun through the trees,
You came to love me.
Like a leaf on the breeze,
You blew away.

Through autumn's golden gown,
We used to kick our way.
You always loved this time of year.
Those fallen leaves lie undisturbed now,
'Cause you're not here.

A gentle rain falls softly on my weary eyes,
As if to hide a lonely tear.
My life will be forever autumn,
Now you're not here.

Amy Louise Warr (12)
Pensnett School of Technology, Brierley Hill

Bullying Poem

1 pound, 2 pound, 3 pound, 4
He's had my money, why does he want more?
5 pound, 6 pound, now it's 7
8 pound, 9 pound, 10 pound and 11.

They took my shoes and my Rolex
I asked, 'Dear Lord, what's going to happen next?'
They took my new tie and my coat
They put it in the pool and watched it float.

I come to school, it's always the same
Picked on by people with no brain
On Tuesday it gets really bad
By Friday I am truly sad.

I went into the classroom
He looked into my eye
I looked into his eye
Then I looked and wondered why, why, why?

He tried to get more money off me
The head teacher walked in and I shouted, 'Mr Fee!'
He went to the office and I laughed at him
I've got my own back
He won't be back for a while
And that's a fact!

Kyle Smith (12)
Pensnett School of Technology, Brierley Hill

Anthony Slater And Chris Baggott

A nyone knows my name, it is Anthony Slater
N an, I will see you later
T oday I saw an alligator
H ey, Shannon, see you later, alligator
O h my God I forgot my homework
N o, I got to finish my class work
Y esterday I finished my coursework and homework.

S hannon is my sister
L ater I will buy a dragster
A nyone up for a faster run than yesterday?
T oday I go to Devon
E ven get up at seven
R ising sun down in Devon.

A t three I go to Great Yarmouth
N an is going to Exmouth
D ad is going to Caister Beach holiday park.

C hris is the man
H e turns on the fan
R iding our motorbikes
I n the campsite with two trikes
S triking a rod took by a pike.

B uying stuff for our fishing stuff
A nd we go round tricking teachers
G ot to go picking apples
G oing down Merry Hill
O h
T oday is my birthday
T omorrow it's Monday.

Anthony Slater (12)
Pensnett School of Technology, Brierley Hill

Bullying

Every day it's all the same
I get called nasty names
They have a song that goes like this
One, two they come for you
Three, four they throw you up a wall
Five, six they have nasty tricks
Seven, eight you're their bait
Nine, ten you're covered in phlegm
Or they sing this
You're up the wall at the count of four
They're after you in the count of two
Their nasty tricks are at six
You're their mate at the count of eight
And it's time to phlegm at ten
They punch
They kick
At lunch
And they come in a bunch
Ready to crunch
You may cry
You may scream
It'll make you dream
And they have a team
You won't want to come to school
They won't even learn to leave
They hang around the mall
They have a dog that loves to drool
And they love to go to Linley Hall.

Andrew Turner (12)
Pensnett School of Technology, Brierley Hill

What . . . ?

The anger flows through my veins,
As the tears trickle down my face.
Tired of being stuck in my non-existing Hell,
Scared to move in case I break,
Or break someone else.
The sickness of the problems that shadow my life,
Linger around my body, get printed on my memory,
And become cremated with my soul.

My heart is fragile like a feather, as if it was made,
Destined to break.
The open wounds created by living around the people I love,
Hate and fear,
Bleed with the lies that they fed me,
And ache for the peace that my hand reaches out for,
But is always just out of my grasp.

I am showered with lies that are here to 'protect' me from
        the truth.
But how can I be protected from what I already know?
From what I know and from what I see
From the enemy that should be loathed and forgotten,
From me . . .

Michelle Payne (13)
Pensnett School of Technology, Brierley Hill

Fishing

F ishing is good
 I t's something that's good to do
S natch the fish
H ook the fish
 I t's a big fish
N o cheating
G ood luck.

Ben Fellows (12)
Pensnett School of Technology, Brierley Hill

There Was A Man

There was a man from Wales
His head was a big as a whale
If you'd touch him he'd squall
His name is the bigheaded Dale.

There was a man from Spain
Who works on a very big crane
One day he had a cough
And he fell right off
And that sent him very insane.

There was a man from Denmark
Who used to be scared of the dark
He met Sue
Who'll go with you
So they went off down the park.

Thomas Griffiths (13)
Pensnett School of Technology, Brierley Hill

Cats And Dogs

C an we stop people killing them?
A nd why do they hurt them?
T ell someone about it!
S top the killings!

A nd they are hurting dogs!
N ever keep it away from people helping!
D o you love dogs and cats?

D on't throw them up the wall!
O pen the door and let them out.
G uard your dogs like they guard you.
S ome people kill them for fun!

Sara Davies (13)
Pensnett School of Technology, Brierley Hill

Boring School!

I hate being at school
Everyone treats me as a fool.
I try to have a laugh
Until I go to Maths.

I made a new friend called Jade
She taught me how to use a spade.
I met another friend called Billie
She is so soft and so silly.
I met another friend called Steph
She always hangs around with Beth.

It turned quarter past three
I go home for my tea
But there's always school tomorrow.

Hollie Nixon (13)
Pensnett School of Technology, Brierley Hill

Christopher

C hris, he's the man
H e turns on the fan
R iding our motorbikes
I n the campsite on our trikes
S triking a rod took by a pike
T oday I'm going to play football
O n the wing to see the king
P arty all night
H e's to see a fight
E ven I get up at seven
R ising sun in Devon.

Christopher Baggott (14)
Pensnett School of Technology, Brierley Hill

Teacher's Pest

There was this boy who was a pain
Who ended up in detention every day
The teachers thought bring back the cane
For our little pest, our little Jay.

He kicked and punched everyone he saw
Jay was a real pain in the bum
Once he got one of the teachers to head butt him to the floor
He looked really clever but really he was dumb.

His hands were like two giant claws
His imagination was way over the top
He would never stop for a short pause
His exam results went down into a big drop.

Stephanie Hughes (13)
Pensnett School of Technology, Brierley Hill

A Fighting Friend

There was a time when I fought
In the hay the man I fought
Said I looked pretty gay. I smacked
Him in the mouth and he fell down south.
He banged his head on the solid concrete
Floor, then sat back up and said he can't
Take anymore. Nowadays I sit on the
Stacks of hay, seeing him once again
Feeding his pet hen. If he started again
I would punch him there and then. Now he
Doesn't say nothing to me, no one would
Think that it could be, that the boy
On the farm could fall and break his knee.

Martin Stevens (16)
Pensnett School of Technology, Brierley Hill

Cinderella

Cinderella lost her slipper,
In return she found a nipper.
Cinderella now in bed,
Accidentally banged her head.
Cinderella found her slipper,
By a handsome, charming kipper.

Cinderella had not a clue,
Stuck it on with super glue.
Cinderella is now upset,
Lost her one and only pet.
Cinderella is now blue,
Along with the ugly two.

Cinderella can't ignore,
Opening the big, brown door.
Cinderella washes clothes,
As her face is as red as a rose.
Cinderella now scrubs the floor,
And has to listen to her stepsister's roar.

Cinderella is now calm,
As they whisper Prince Charm.
Cinderella lost her dream,
As she went off like cream.
Cinderella not in love,
Flew off like a dove.

Racheal Smallwood (13)
Pensnett School of Technology, Brierley Hill

My Imaginary Friend

My imaginary friend is cool,
He sits on my TV like a fool.
Every morning he wakes me up,
Whacking me with a cup.
His name is Billy,
He acts so silly.

My imaginary friend is small,
He laughs at me because I'm tall.
All he eats is mouldy eggs,
And wakes up with wobbly legs.
He talks to me till midnight,
I say shut up and he gives me a fright.

My imaginary friend speaks posh,
When I say, 'Ah,' he says, 'Gosh!'
When I go out he acts good,
Hiding in my jumper hood.
He listens to my music beats,
And says, 'Come on, pull up a seat.'

My imaginary friend wants all my stuff,
My cats, mobile phone, I just puff.
He says I'm silly,
But not like him Billy.
I will get him back soon,
When he comes from the moon.

My imaginary friend has gone,
When he comes back I'll have done.
I lost him when I took him to school,
That'll show him not to be such a fool.

Laura Danielle Cooper (14)
Pensnett School of Technology, Brierley Hill

My Dog

My big, beautiful dog,
He is lovely like a log.

My dog is cute and caring,
And he is always staring.

My big, beautiful dog,
He is lovely like a log.

His claws are sharp,
And his eyes are dark.

My big, beautiful dog,
He is lovely like a log.

When my mom walks around the place,
He follows at the same pace.

My big, beautiful dog,
He is lovely like a log.

He wags his long tail,
Which is as thin as a skinny nail.

My big, beautiful dog,
He is lovely like a log.

Sarah Russon (13)
Pensnett School of Technology, Brierley Hill

Short Poem For You

I like bananas
They make me wear pyjamas.

I like grapes
They make me feel great.

Best of all I like dates
Because I have lots of mates.

Katie Felton (12)
Pensnett School of Technology, Brierley Hill

Football

On the pitch it's full of grime
At the end you look at the time
When you put the ball in the goal
You do a fabulous goal.

On the field I score a hat trick
Then I see a player pass it slip
When the ref blows for a foul
All the crowd start to howl.

When the ball gets put in the net
It gets wrapped up, the goal is set
When the player gave a kick
It was in the net like a hat trick.

When the ball hit the post
It started to burn like hot toast
When the player was on the list
He was annoyed when he broke his wrist.

Steven Cartwright (13)
Pensnett School of Technology, Brierley Hill

Scott's Fringe

Scott's fringe looks like a ski jump
He needs to calm it down
It's far too big for the rooms
And too extreme says Miss Plume
When he has white hair
It will be the next holiday resort!

Tom Bradley (13)
Pensnett School of Technology, Brierley Hill

Lads

I love to flirt with lads,
My boyfriend is so sad,
He doesn't get along with many dads,
Especially my old dad
But he doesn't think my mom is so bad.

I had a friend who wanted him,
I went so sad and down and deeply dim,
He went to my school,
I always see him in the hall.

He never comes up the mall,
He is very tall,
He isn't the best looking of them all,
He was the chap that I always falled for!

Samantha Griffiths (13)
Pensnett School of Technology, Brierley Hill

My Boyfriend Nick

I have a boyfriend called Nick
He was a good one to pick.
He has a nice smile
We're going to out for a while.
He has beautiful eyes
He doesn't eat many pies.
He has a really nice giggle
He also has a sexy wiggle.
He's got a really nice body
He doesn't really like Noddy.
I love everything about him
He's certainly not dim.

Danielle D'Rozario (14)
Pensnett School of Technology, Brierley Hill

My Pet

My pet is small and cute,
He is so cool I wouldn't give him the boot.

My pet is called Dwayne,
But sometimes he can be a pain.

My pet is black and white,
He will definitely give you a fright.

My pet hates all strangers he sees,
But he loves to eat honeybees.

My pet is a cat,
But he is not fat.

My pet likes to sleep,
Make sure he does not peep.

Jamie Raine (13)
Pensnett School of Technology, Brierley Hill

My Mom Is A Saint

My mom's a saint,
She's like my little mate.
She cooks me meals,
And she buys me good deals.
She can drive me round the bend,
She can also make amends.
She likes someone called Denny,
But she's going out with Lenny.
She's never got any money,
And she's got a pet bunny.
So don't be funny,
She's only me mummy.

Marie Leddington (13)
Pensnett School of Technology, Brierley Hill

Chocolate's For Women!

Chocolate, something to die for,
It makes you want so much more.
Chocolate isn't a deadly sin,
You don't want to throw it in the bin.
Chocolate is made for women,
When we eat it while wrapped in black satin.
Chocolate is better than any other crap,
It makes you want to have a nap.
Chocolate has a mouth-watering melt,
For when we have our cramps.
The best are those scrumptious king-size bars,
Which they are trying to ban.
We all know why, because of that man.
We all have our really bad days,
And have a chocolate as it melts on our tongue.
The time it takes just so long,
As we listen to a romantic song.
Chocolate, chocolate, no need to waste,
Chocolate, chocolate with its great taste.

Hayley Coates (15)
Pensnett School of Technology, Brierley Hill

Dream

Every night I have a dream.
But sometimes I wake with a scream.
Sometimes I am really bad.
And most of the time people think I'm mad.
I wake up with good dreams of cookies.
Most of the time they are of stinging bees.

Mitchell R Hale (13)
Pensnett School of Technology, Brierley Hill

Baggies' Bad Day

With the Baggies with a defeat
With a ref who is a cheat
The ball is in the Baggies' net
Baggies going to lose you can bet!

With the team being hurt
You're special if you're wearing the number one shirt
With the score at one-nil
We're disadvantaged playing on a hill.

With us playing bad
Making us and the supporters sad
With us losing the FA Cup
We certainly won't be going up.

With Kumas shown the red card
The Baggies not on their guard.

Steven Priest (13)
Pensnett School of Technology, Brierley Hill

I Had No Mates

I had no mates
I was a Larry Loner
I was a little, sweet girl without any dates
I decided to be a blood donor.

I finally had a mate
We played night and day
She decided to leave me and go out the gate
When she finally left she told me her name
She was Fay.

Jodie Handley (14)
Pensnett School of Technology, Brierley Hill

My Mr Right

We were friends for a little while,
He touched my heart with his charming smile.
I fell for his charmed love.

As his hand touched my heart,
I know this feeling will last forever.
My heart loves to beat when we are together.

Romantic walks in the park,
Walks through the dark,
Meeting in the starlight,
And now I know I have found
My beloved Mr Right.

Stacey Pyatt (13)
Pensnett School of Technology, Brierley Hill

Shaney's Tale

I found an old handbag
And I filled it with lead
I hit an old lady
On top of the head.

The policeman he caught me
And he asked me my name
I gave him my answer
With a bicycle chain.

Now come, dear Shaney
Come wipe up your tears
You're going to Borstal
For three long years!

Shane Simmonds (13)
Pensnett School of Technology, Brierley Hill

Football

On the pitch you look at the time
Then you fall over in that messy grime
You do a forward roll
When you put it in the goal.

On the pitch you score a hat-trick
Then I see a player pass it slip
The crowd starts to howl
When the ref calls for a foul.

The ball gets wrapped up like a pet
When it goes in the net
When the player gave a kick
It was in the net like a tick.

When the ball hits the post
It strutted to burn like toast
When the player was on the list
Then the other player broke his wrist.

Daniel Southall (13)
Pensnett School of Technology, Brierley Hill

War Is Wrong

Lately the war is always on the news,
It's really giving me the blues.
People are dying,
Faces are crying.
There's always fights,
That last through the night.
Bombs are going off,
That causes loads of coughs.

War is wrong!

Lyndon Hawkins (13)
Pensnett School of Technology, Brierley Hill

The Day I Thought I Fell In Love

You asked to meet me in the park
I stood there for hours, alone in the dark
I waited and waited, you never came
I'll never ever forget your name.

You told me you loved me
You told me you cared
But you only said that
Because I was scared.

The day I thought I fell in love
You floated by on the feather of a dove
You glimpsed back and looked at me
I fell in love immediately.

As the next day came near
You asked me to meet you on the pier
We stood there listening to the sea
Where we kissed so tenderly.

It passed me by a week or two
With not even a word from you
You took my heart and left me confused
Making me feel so abandoned, so used.

So I guessed it's the end, we're through
It's time I found someone new
Why did I ever fall for you?

Bethany Coomby (13)
Pensnett School of Technology, Brierley Hill

There Was A Man From Spain

There was a man from Spain
Who used to work on a very big train
He got off the train and fell in the drain
And that was the end of the man from Spain.

Steven Williams (13)
Pensnett School of Technology, Brierley Hill

My Hamster

My darling little hamster
She is as thin as a stick
Her name is Tiggy
And she is very quick.

My darling little hamster
She is so cute
And she can fit in a baby's boot
I love her so much!

My darling little hamster
She is as thin as a pole
She's never bitten me
Why should she?

She is one year and two months old
But we don't need to be told
Every day she comes out in her ball
She is not very tall.

I wish everyone could see her
And she is covered with fur
Sometimes she does not come out
Because she is all tired out.

She is the best hamster in the world!

Hannah Williams (13)
Pensnett School of Technology, Brierley Hill

Six Uses For A Scarf

A wraparound sarong with a pretty bow.
A headscarf for an old lady to sew.
A designer belt o' so stylish
Christina Aguilera, her T-shirt, very childish
A turban for a man, nice and strikey
Simple around the neck, boring but *lord crikey!*

Stacey Whittaker (14)
Pensnett School of Technology, Brierley Hill

How I Fell In Love With A Tiger

Saw a tiger lay on grass
Antelope started to pass
They scrunched up their eyes
And they say bye-byes
They're broken like a piece of heart
They ran like red-hot heat
So hungry they eat meat
They went for a walk
But they do not talk.

They save my life
But he was strife
He got hurt
But the other was on alert
And that's how I fell in love with tiger.

Alicia Rivero-Mackay (13)
Pensnett School of Technology, Brierley Hill

Mr Right

We were friends for a while,
He touched my heart with his lovely smile.
I fell for his charm,
As he touched my arm.
I know this feeling
Will last forever.
My heart skips beats,
When we're together.
Walks through the park,
Romantic films in the dark.
Meeting under the stars at night,
I know now I have found my beguiling Mr Right.

Natalie Cole (13)
Pensnett School of Technology, Brierley Hill

He's The Ref

They say he's blind
They say he's deaf,
But he's in charge
'Cos he's the ref.

He makes defenders
Get their yards,
Gives diving forwards yellow cards.

He gives off sides
Awards free kicks,
He red cards cheats
For dirty tricks.

'Cos he's the ref!

John Dovovan (13)
Pensnett School of Technology, Brierley Hill

Football For Wonder

When you watch a football match
The keeper has got to be able to catch
If they score a wonderful goal
Jump for joy or dig a hole.

If you draw or even lose
The crowd will give you loads of boos
But if you have a good defeat
The other team wouldn't want a repeat.

If there's fighting on the pitch
Don't join in or you'll end up in a ditch
If the ref doesn't give a thing
He deserves a slap or surely something.

Liam Brookes (13)
Pensnett School of Technology, Brierley Hill

My Wild Family!

My mom is a witch,
She'll never switch.
That's a fact,
Not an act.

My dad is a pest,
He was born in a nest.
He has a clever mind,
He is really kind.

My brother is a pain,
He ought to get the cane.
He messes about,
Like a little trout.

And there's me, so beautifully fine,
In a world that's mysteriously mine.
I'm a girl who likes to be wild,
Ever since a little child!

Natasha Lakin (12)
Pensnett School of Technology, Brierley Hill

Cats And Dogs

Cats
Loveable, kind, friendly, fussy
Dogs
Loving, scratching around and always funny
Cats
Curl up in front of the fire like a ball of fluff, always loving
Dogs
They have big, brown eyes too that stare at you, always loving.

Sarah Burgess (13)
Pensnett School of Technology, Brierley Hill

Beans

Beans, beans, beans
Baked beans, buttered beans
Big for lime beans, long, thing string beans
  Those are just a few.

Green beans, black beans
Big, fat kidney beans, red-hot chilli beans
  Jumping beans too.

Red beans, pinto beans
  Don't forget shelly beans.

Last of all, best of all
  I like jelly beans.

Jess Hickman (15)
Pensnett School of Technology, Brierley Hill

Football Poem

I'm so mad
About football.
I kick it about
Like I'm the ball.

I've been playing footy
Since I was a li'l lad,
'Cause now I can score
Without being bad.

It's all about the skill
And if you're brill,
But if you're not
You're still top-notch.

Luke Wright (11)
Pensnett School of Technology, Brierley Hill

Pink!

Pink is the colour of my favourite shoes,
With a pink bow and beads.

Pink is the colour of my best friend's folder,
With stickers all over it.

Pink is the colour of my teacher's pen,
With a little lid.

Pink is the colour of my friend's top,
With numbers on it.

Pink is sometimes the colour of people's hair,
In a long plait dragging on the floor.

Pink is the top half of my room,
And the other half is purple.

Pink are the colours of my clips,
And bobbles that I have in my hair.

Pink is the colour of one of my favourite jumpers,
Which I wear at night when it's cold.

Pink is the colour of my very favourite top,
Which I wear to my parties.

Vanessa Roden (11)
Pensnett School of Technology, Brierley Hill

Friends

You and I are friends . . .
You fight, I fight . . .
You hurt, I hurt . . .
You cry, I cry . . .
You jump off a bridge . . .
I'll miss ya!

Stacey Palmer (14)
Pensnett School of Technology, Brierley Hill

Footy And The Rest

Roars from the stadium, the light on the pitch
A ditch in the ground
Becomes a boot on the ball
The ball in the net
Sends the crowds up
Fans to the ground
Waiting for the best
Away fans travel
Hooligans fight
Footy! Footy!
What more do we watch?
Arms on the armchair
Glued to the TV
Singing songs
Cheering a team on
Kids at school
Wrecking the grass
Arguing who's best
The row begins
It's all over football
Oh footy, footy, footy!

Luke Tibbetts (11)
Pensnett School of Technology, Brierley Hill

Battlefield

An army came marching to war
That's what we all saw
With their uniform and boots
Ready to shoot
So we ran over a hill
While they kill
And then we went away
So we lived 'til another day.

Joe Tibbetts (11)
Pensnett School of Technology, Brierley Hill

Evie May

Evie May was born on the 4th of May,
And she was quite big and heavy,
Ever since then she has brightened my day,
And made us all very happy!

That's my baby sister, she is a little cutie,
She's only 5 months old, but she's a little beauty!
She's active and happy, smiley and cheerful,
And in a few months time, will be a right handful!

Evie May is ever so cute,
And she loves it when you go toot, toot!
She dribbles like a drain on a wet, rainy day!
But she's a very special girl because she's my Evie May!

Alice Laurie (12)
Pensnett School of Technology, Brierley Hill

Hallowe'en

Pumpkins alight
Giving you a fright
Ghosts are creeping
Whilst the frogs are leaping
The vampires lurk
While the witches smirk
The wolves howl
Whilst the ordinary dogs growl
Zombies stumble
The mummies mumble
The skeletons rattle their bones
While the black cats moan
I'm terrified of Hallowe'en
I'm not staying on my own!

Sarah Woods & Kimberly Palmer (12)
Pensnett School of Technology, Brierley Hill

Eye Of The Tiger Vs Eye Of The Falcon

Eye of the tiger a prowling and mysterious beast
That destroys the land that's full of lies.

Eye of the falcon, the sharp eye that can catch light,
They pursue the fight.

The eye of the tiger with the eye of the falcon,
Together they could destroy the world
Or they could save it.
The tiger, the falcon,
If they fought they would be far from welcome.
Slash! go the beasts,
Now their decision is to feast.

Haydn Williams (11)
Pensnett School of Technology, Brierley Hill

My Mother

My mother
Is like no other.
Kind and sweet
With very soft feet.

My mother
Is like no other.
With brown, long hair
And very, very fair.

My mother
Is like no other
Because I said
She's my favourite mother.

Hannah Humphries (11)
Pensnett School of Technology, Brierley Hill

Water And Sea

There are lots of things you can do with water.
You can swim or go surfing out to sea,
You can go home and leave it 'til later.
It's better than hanging out in a tree!

While hot spring waters are calming,
Fear! Some sharks are alarming!
River rapids are good to ride,
If you're a thrill-seeker.
See if you can beat the tide!
If you're going to sea don't be a reeker!
Would *you* go to sea and have fun
Or catch a tan with the sun?

Luke Hadley (11)
Pensnett School of Technology, Brierley Hill

Attack From Behind

Silent, silent everywhere
Nothing to be seen
It all happened in a rush
Bang! It hit me from behind
What was it? rushed through my head
Then I looked up
It gleamed me in the eye.
'What are you?'
It replied, 'A tiger.'
With his sharp claw he took a swoop
It hit me from behind.

Adam Jukes (11)
Pensnett School of Technology, Brierley Hill

England

England are good, they are great,
They are fearless and fearless is their motto.
Wembley is their stadium,
Their stadium it will be.
They have excellent players like David Beckham and me.
And this is how they score:

James to Neville to Cole to Lampard,
Then we score a goal.
After one it becomes two goals then three goals.
Three-nil - winners, that's what England are.
They're in the top half of the chart.

Joe Lawley (11)
Pensnett School of Technology, Brierley Hill

Goal!

When you put the ball in the goal
You do an exuberant roll.
When the ref saw this great team
He needed to believe what he had seen.

When the ref gave a free-kick
The ball was in the net like a lick.
The players were getting hungry
They had decided on victory.

Darren Hill (14)
Pensnett School of Technology, Brierley Hill

My Street

Every day cars go by
Children always cry
Banging and bouncing balls
And then Mom calls
People running and jumping
In the street
They only come in just for a treat
When moms and dads call them in
Look at you, just like a bin.

Amanda Morris
Pensnett School of Technology, Brierley Hill

My Dog

My dog's called Gilbert, I am called Jack
My dog's got four legs, I've got two
My dog's got black ears, I've got white
My dog's got paws, I've got hands
My dog's a Staff, I am a human being.

Jack Bedford (11)
Pensnett School of Technology, Brierley Hill

Heaven Poem!

Heaven is a wondrous creation above,
Which is what brings us on this Earth to love.
Angels with wings, harps and strings,
You will never destruct the joy it brings.

Sunyia Tahir (14)
Pensnett School of Technology, Brierley Hill

Video Games

Video games are really cool
Don't mock them 'cos they rule
With the GameCube the Xbox and the PS2
The only time you'll stop playing is to go to the loo!

With games like Jak and Daxter, Mario and The Sims
You'll need a supply of food like crisps and tins.

Adam Copson (12)
Pensnett School of Technology, Brierley Hill

Mountain Bikes

I go mountain biking.
I love mountain bikes.
I go every Sunday.
I have a Marin.
I go to Cannock.
I go in the car.
I have a hell of a time.
Then I have McDonald's and it's all, all mine!

Sam Barnbrook (12)
Pensnett School of Technology, Brierley Hill

Rainbows

Colours are bright colours are like colours of the rainbow.
The rainbow glistens in the sky when the sun is shining
And the weather is raining.

When the sun shines off some oil
It also looks like the rainbow.

Brett Wood (12)
Pensnett School of Technology, Brierley Hill

Our Tree

Swaying
    As branches do
Back and forth,
    Leaves shaking -
        Vigorously.

Our tree dominates the landscape
It stretches and moans, the wind
    Beats through its matted leaves.
Through secured windows I watch our tree
    Take a thrashing.

The branches begin to split.

Stubbornly it stands there, like some colossal animal
    That just won't be moved.
    Defiant!
Our tree in our yard, looming, dark as ever.
Maybe it will beat the storm, maybe -
A crack!
It illuminates the sky, our menacing tree split
    Right down the middle.
It's all burned out, our tree, our yard, our love.

Jay-Dee Johnson (15)
Perryfields High School, Oldbury

Blue Moon

Once upon a blue moon
The shadows rose
For the shadows are alive
They hate the light
And love the dark
For evil can pose.

They fight for one
And die for all.
When darkness falls
Light shall emerge.
For people fight for the light.
Shadows do it by dying.
They destroy it by living.

Light conquered evil
With minimum power
While that happened
In shadow's final hour
They went to battle
So it was unfinished.

Jamie Coleman (13)
Perryfields High School, Oldbury

The Commentary

Hello and welcome to
This packed Mardson Square flat
Where Alan and Craig are
To play this footy match.

Alan to start, shoots, oh
He's hit the compost heap
Craig now on the attack
Shimmies the tree, shoots, scores.

What can Alan do now?
He runs, takes him on, shoots
Yes! 1-1. Craig volleys, no
He has smashed a window.

No one's in, that is lucky
Alan's still but he's shot
What a great save from Craig
Craig now turns Alan, horrid.

Alan gives him no choice
The ref has given a pen
Craig hits it, he scores again
2-1 to Craig. He's fine.

Alan in the last minute
Takes on Craig, shoots, 2 all
What a great game of footy
There goes the full time whistle.

Louis Bridges (13)
Perryfields High School, Oldbury

What Happened To The Place?

The world was ruined
By people who damage the place.
Why do people do this?

People kill
People hate
People fight
So what are we going to do?

We'll stop the fights
Stop the hate
Stop the killing
All we've got to do is love each other.

When the world's a better place
Loads of people will love everyone
In the world.

Rachael Elizabeth Healey (13)
Perryfields High School, Oldbury

All Mixed Up

I feel like I'm on top of the world.
I feel good and special.
I feel like my life's worthwhile.
I feel as happy as can be.
I feel like the person I used to know as me.

I feel bad and ever so sad.
I feel dull.
I feel like I'm lost, all alone.
I feel like the sun, hidden in shade.
I feel like this person, the one that I've made.

I feel as angry as can be.
I feel red with rage and mad.
I feel like a tiger locked in a cage.
I feel so frustrated.

I feel angry, happy and sad.

Carly-Marie Talbot (14)
Queen Mary's High School, Walsall

Mortals

Because all that I see before me is
Maddening,
Putrefying,
So that even before entering
Innocence is spoiled,
I fear immortality,
In which decadence is worshipped,
And all true belief is lost to a false body.

I can no longer follow orders,
As I am blind in darkness, the reincarnation of light.

Relieve me of this sin,
And hold me in hands of purity,
As I have already drunk from the goblet of temptation,
Of which the poison has already corrupted my soul.

I'm running through the darkness,
In sheer enjoyment,
And cannot stop.

Its intoxicating elixir pulsates through and through,
Drowning me in its evil.

I have no other path,
Now that my innocence and purity have been swallowed,
Relieve me from this sin before it deeply embeds itself.

Ramanpreet Kaur Jassel (15)
Queen Mary's High School, Walsall

Young Love

Hearts as light as feathers, in a summer breeze,
Struck by Cupid's arrows, wandering with ease,
Whispering sweet nothings, because young love always lasts,
Not seeing past tomorrow, when the truth might come at last.

Harbouring the secrets, of a broken heart,
Watching lovers kissing, reluctant to pull apart.
Everybody seeks it, everlasting love,
The one who is our soul mate, sent from up above.

God has our lives mapped out, from one moment to the next,
Looking down upon us, planning out what's best.
We're fated to fall in love, what must be, must be,
Blinded by the moment, finding lock and key.

But the key doesn't fit, the lock is tightly closed,
Young love becomes too painful, raw emotions felt and froze.
Now older and wiser, we try to warn the rest,
Young lovers just ignore us, think they know what's best.

They tell us we're preaching, we need to 'mind our own',
They just want to be happy, consequences unknown.
You hope that it will work out, an everlasting flame,
Not yet to be stamped out, and others take the blame.

Those of us unlucky, to seek that love again,
Only find the embers, the young think we're insane.

So in a shadowed corner, we watch with broken hearts,
Wishing back that feeling, not knowing where to start.

Samantha Johnson (15)
Queen Mary's High School, Walsall

You

Look back on that which you had engraved on your slate,
Borrowed from another who came before.
Trod up the same ladders that were laid out for you,
Prepared for you,
Left for you.
So that you would know exactly where to tread on your path.

Trundle along through insecurity -
Debate the insignificance of what
Your own existence was.
Contemplate whether you missed yourself too much to let you go.
You'll find me still keeping your memory warm,
Subconsciously arguing with your mind as to
Who was the better you?

Write your story down, on pages faded old,
Printed through generations;
A memento of yourself who came before you.
Step forward into your new face,
Staring down through my eyes at my hands, now your hands. And,
Alienated, I'll smile your smile,

And greet you with a sign, that you made,
Gave the undisputable demand for design, welcoming yourself
As she who will take over.
And then, I'll look back when I grow,
And I'll write my story,

Leaving out anything that I wanted to say.

Stephanie Jackson (16)
Queen Mary's High School, Walsall

The Fallen

In a trance I climb the stairs.
I slowly ascend to his lair.
I know that I should run away,
But some power makes me stay.

I walk along the landing floor.
I do not know what is in store.
My hand upon a door knob turns.
What's inside I soon shall learn.

I see a man with midnight hair,
And his skin so pale and fair.
He stands beside a windowpane.
The moon it shines around his frame.

He fixes his eyes upon my own,
And I'm enraptured by his tone.
He coaxes me into his embrace,
And from my neck removes the lace.

His breath upon my neck feels hot.
I have no power to make him stop.
A sudden pain and I know no more,
Until I next wake upon the floor.

I'm now a creature of the night,
Who'll never again see the sun's light,
So by his side I shall stay,
And never see the light of day.

Charlotte Askew (17)
Queen Mary's High School, Walsall

Time Travels To Paris!

I was threatened, anxious,
Excited
On my way at last
On my way at last
Freezing, dark 2am stop,
I'm glowing like a lighthouse!
But I'm on my way at last
Motorbike, amusements
Brumm brumm
200mph - imagination steaming me to France!
Coach at a stop.
Dead end!
'Dead End' service station
Coach dead
Children walking dead
Time - travel to Paris
Held on 'pause' like a pc game.

Samuel Archer (11)
Ridgewood High School, Stourbridge

Children In Need

When you're rhyming along with me
Just remember the Children In Need
I know this poem doesn't mean much
But some children don't even eat lunch

What a shame when you think
That those kids can hardly drink
I mean, come on people, give some cash
You might be shocked, but they dash
Towards the food that you send
With 30 pounds, that's all you spend!

Lucy Pilkington (12)
Waseley Hills High School, Birmingham

Best Friends

Me and Lucy
We are best friends
And we will stay that way
Until the end.
We use the super glue
To keep us together
We will still be best friends
Forever and ever.
Even when we're older
We'll still be mates
Even when
We're on our first dates.
We want to live in a flat
We'll even have a welcome mat.
So this is what I've said
Without a doubt
We're best friends
And that's what it's all about.

Aimee Bates (12)
Waseley Hills High School, Birmingham

The Snowy Day

I like the winter
When it snows
When everything's white
It's like balls of cotton wool.
When the ponds freeze
With the fire breeze
When you have snowball fights
On a cold night
Your hands go blue
Before you knew.

Adam Richards (15)
Whiteheath Pupil Referral Unit, Rowley Regis

Summer Love

We had a holiday romance,
I thought you would keep in touch,
I can't believe you lost your chance,
You can't have liked me much.

You will always be in my heart,
I can't say you feel the same way,
Even though we are apart,
My feelings for you are here to stay.

We spent all our holiday together,
I phoned you everyday,
I thought it would last forever,
But things didn't go that way.

I've cried over you,
But no tears will fall anymore,
I smiled, thinking of you,
But they faded when you closed the door.

You have caused me so much pain and grief,
I've wasted my time loving you,
So here I am turning over a new leaf,
I believe you have too.

Jane Farmer (15)
Whiteheath Pupil Referral Unit, Rowley Regis

Guitars Rock

They're all different shapes,
They're all different makes.
They make all different noises
When they're plugged in the amp.
Some of them are cool,
Some of them are camp,
Gibson and Fender are some of the makes
You can even get some that look like snakes.

Matthew Miccolls (15)
Whiteheath Pupil Referral Unit, Rowley Regis

Seasons

I love the summer
I love the spring
I love when the birds flutter and sing
The winter's harsh and wet and cold
But I will always love the snow
The autumn leaves are red and gold
They float to the ground when the trees get cold.
I love all of the seasons
They're very special to me
You see, if we didn't have them
Where would we be?

Alicia Biggs (15)
Whiteheath Pupil Referral Unit, Rowley Regis

My Music

I like music
Especially loud music
Music that makes your
Heart jump and your
Ears ring.
Music that makes you
Want to shout and scream.
Music with a heavy booming sound
Music that makes your
Neighbours angry.
This is the music I like.

Stephen Brooks (15)
Whiteheath Pupil Referral Unit, Rowley Regis

A Dog's Life

From head to tail,
From the ears down to the nail.
Beautiful eyes, friendly and cute
Tatty and ruined, that's the state of my new boot!

Her teeth, well what can I say?
You wouldn't want to meet her on a nasty day.
Her fur, silky and brown
Makes people stop when we walk through town.

At six years old
She still does what she's told.
She's one of a kind,
And that's hard to find!

I've got to go now and take her for a walk,
I'm glad we had this quick talk.
We'll have to do it again one day,
What do you say about next May?

Samantha Marston (14)
William Bradford Community College, Earl Shilton, Leicester

Clouds

C louds are everywhere
L ying around without a care
O ut of this world, out of this air
U p above the world so high
D own and up like a beady eye
S itting watching the clouds go up, up in the sky.

Ruth Shred (14)
William Bradford Community College, Earl Shilton, Leicester

Lonely

When I look at the sky
I always wonder why
You seem to pass me by
I just want to cry.

I can't hide my feelings inside
Why do we always divide
You're always looking at another guy
But why?

Why can't we solve
The problems that are cold
It's too late now
I don't care anymore.

The love of ours was false
Now I can see this
I don't need you anymore
Goodbye . . .

Craig Lawson (14)
William Bradford Community College, Earl Shilton, Leicester

Dreaming

Everybody dreams
About realistic things
Maybe even fantasy
Like flying pigs with wings.

You could dream of anything
Whatever is on your mind
Lots of money or chocolate cake.
Dreams are made for people
Everybody gets them.

Lucy Hyde (14)
William Bradford Community College, Earl Shilton, Leicester

Racing For 1st

They all get to the starting positions,
With their engines roaring
Roaring as loud as a lion
Waiting for the lights to go out.

4 . . .
3 . . .
2 . . .
1 . . .

And the lights have gone out
They are racing down to the first corner
Racing for first place.

Bumpers hitting bumpers
Racers spinning off
Crowd screaming
Wheels screeching
Lap by lap by lap
Number sixty-nine crosses the finish line
The chequered flag is waved.

Stephen Blighton (14)
William Bradford Community College, Earl Shilton, Leicester

Stars

Stars live way up high above
And come out only at night
They stand out in the pitch-black sky,
Because they're extremely bright!

I wish one day a star would fall
Right down here to the floor.
I would catch it with my own bare hands
And treasure it for evermore!

Chloe Golding (14)
William Bradford Community College, Earl Shilton, Leicester

Racism In Football

It's always the same
In that popular game,
Just one racist remark
It acts like a spark
The fire alight
And the players in sight
The fists are flying
But the fire's not dying,
The card has been shown
But the fire's not been blown
The fire will keep going
If the racism keeps growing
As long as racism is here
It's the fire we all must fear,
If the hooligans are shouting
The fire is not doubting,
That its power is thriving
Because the racism's not subsiding.

Jake Hines (14)
William Bradford Community College, Earl Shilton, Leicester

Hopeless

Lying down in the damp mud
Looking into the scope
Seeing the green sea coming towards us
Taking everyone out in its path.
Everyone shouting, 'Gas! Gas!'
Seeing people drowning
Choking to death
Nowhere to go
Nowhere to hide
Hopeless!

Nicholas Ordish (14)
William Bradford Community College, Earl Shilton, Leicester

Watch Your Back

Watch out for the dude on the run from the psychiatric ward
His face is up for capture, with a reward
He'll beat you up don't be fooled by his looks
Quicker than you talk, you'll be caught by his hooks
He'll rip you to shreds
You'll be in your final bed.

Watch your back wherever you are
If you don't you will end up with more than a scar.

Tell all your family about this evil man
He will grow and recruit his evil clan
Families all around are reaching the end
To be fair, this is becoming a bit of a trend
Many compare him to a human killing flea
No need to worry, he won't catch me!

Watch your back wherever you are
If you don't you will end up with more than a scar.

One night I was chilling, having a bud
The next thing I knew I was covered in blood
The last thing I saw was a knocked over beer
All around screaming was all I could hear
Suddenly I was deafened, then I received the final whack
That was me gone, it all went dark black.

Watch your back wherever you may be
Otherwise you will end up dead . . . like me!

Harry Fish (14)
William Bradford Community College, Earl Shilton, Leicester

Silent Lion

The lion stalks its prey;
Its eyes sharp, its sound soft
Silent and deadly.
The prey is oblivious,
It wanders the land,
The lion waits for the moment
Pounces. Wounds. Kills.

The prey emerges,
From the dust, smoke and fire,
Its face black as night.
From a wounded head, the blood streaming.
The sirens sound all around the prey.
Crashes of debris all around, the alarm's deafening.
The prey is down.
The lion has pounced.

The faces of the prey are not the only victims
The silent bomb has hit,
The silent bomb has shocked.
They prey is cautious
The prey watches and listens.

We are vulnerable,
We are the prey
We are cautious
We watch and we listen
Are we safe?
Or is the silent lion still on top.

Oliver Julian (14)
William Bradford Community College, Earl Shilton, Leicester

Where Are My Teeth!

I've lost my teeth, they've run away
I don't know where they've gone
They've done a runner, I had no say
That dentist was a con.

I cannot find them anywhere
They've vanished out of sight
Nicked by thin air
Stolen by night.

I cannot chew
I cannot talk
I only had two
I sound like a dork.

Oh here they are
They hadn't gone
I tell you what
I'd lose my head
If it weren't screwed on!

Daniel Holder (14)
William Bradford Community College, Earl Shilton, Leicester

Motorbike

Motorbike, lonely and unused.
Stashed in the darkness, unloved and abused.
Silently waiting for love and care.
No one can be bothered, no time, no love, no care.
All dusty and dirty, entrapped in the dark.
Covered in cobwebs, spiders are crawling.
No engine a' roaring
No bodywork glow.
Let's get this engine running, and see how she goes.

Joshua Grove (14)
William Bradford Community College, Earl Shilton, Leicester

The Four Seasons

Spring is the time when new animals are born
Spring is the time when it's light at dawn
Spring is when new flowers grow
Spring is when the daffodils show.

Summer is the time when the sun is strong
Summer is the time when the days are long
Summer is when we splash in the sea
Summer is when a bee stings me.

Autumn is the time when it starts to get cold
Autumn is the time when the leaves turn gold
Autumn is the time when the frost's on the ground
Autumn is when Jack Frost is around.

Winter is the time when everything's white
Winter is the time when the snow's in sight
Winter is when it's freezing cold
Winter is when it's not good to be bald.

Louise Hamilton (14)
William Bradford Community College, Earl Shilton, Leicester

Football

Football you can scream and shout
Football you can run about
Football you can play anywhere
Football is a man's game
Football is very rough
Football is hard and tough
Football is for boys, not girls
Football is a man's game
Football you can kick a ball
Football you can make a wall
Football you can be quite tall
Football, football, football.

Luke Hancock (14)
William Bradford Community College, Earl Shilton, Leicester

Alone

You feel lost, alone, isolated, without even another soul present.
You walk down to the shore where you once stood together before.
Your heart skips a beat as you remember times past, back when
you thought the love you had would last.
The happy memories bring a tear to your eye
You crouch down; take a look up at the sky and watch the clouds
                                                    float past.
Without a care in the world you would lean back into his arms
and exchange a smile.
You never thought that you would be alone.
You never thought that it would end up this way,
But that, my friend, is one of the disasters war brings.

Hollie Smith (14)
William Bradford Community College, Earl Shilton, Leicester

Love - Friendship

Love is like a flower
It starts out as a grain
Then it begins to bloom.
When the flower has finished blooming
It will stay true and secure for a while
Then the flower will soon die.
Love is like a flower.

The journey of true friendship is like the odyssey of the ocean
It begins its travels as a bubbling spring
And full of potential develops into a stream
The stream then advances on into a river,
Finally the river carries on, expanding into the ocean.
The journey of true friendship is like the odyssey of the ocean,
It just keeps on improving and then carries on and on.

Rebecca Whawell (15)
William Bradford Community College, Earl Shilton, Leicester

Untitled

I can't believe I did it
I don't believe I tried
After I had done it
I sat there and cried.

Now life has come around
And now I feel much better
That's why I'm writing a poem
Not a suicide letter.

When life gets you down
Talk to a friend
Because they will be with you
Until the very end.

I'm writing this poem
Just to let people know
No matter how bad life gets
Never let your life go!

Rebecca Lally (14)
William Bradford Community College, Earl Shilton, Leicester

Rugby

Fifteen players standing tall
Fifteen players playing with a ball.

Five players standing in a trench
Five players are sitting on the bench.

Two players are extremely cold
Two players are very bold.

One player is as thin as a stick
One player is as hard as a brick.

Three for a kick, five for a try
Look! As the ball flies through the sky.

William Lawrence (14)
William Bradford Community College, Earl Shilton, Leicester

Winter

It's getting cold,
It's hard to sleep
When your toes are cold
And you start to weep.

You sniffle and snuffle
Your nose keeps on running
The good thing is the snow is stunning
Running around in the snow all day
Watching the children, loving to play.

All the birds are making their nest
And all the children are trying their best
To enjoy their day
In every way
Getting wet and covered with snow
And then when it is time to go
They snuggle up in a warm bed
With a hot water bottle under their head
They wake the next day, ready to play
But the snow has gone
And your nose starts to run.

Holly Ball (14)
William Bradford Community College, Earl Shilton, Leicester

Football

The ball was kicked up in the air,
And flew with the greatest of ease,
It went through the posts and the game was
Won and everyone was pleased.

Celebrations went on for hours on end,
Until everyone was drunk
Later on the ref came in
And said we hadn't won!

Guy Lucas (15)
William Bradford Community College, Earl Shilton, Leicester

Love

Love is like a flower
Not to be trodden
Love is like a name
Not to be forgotten.

Love is like a forest
Blooming in the sun
Love is like a journey
Only just begun.

Some take love for granted
And treat it really bad
But until you've lost it
You don't know what you've had.

Elanor Martin (14)
William Bradford Community College, Earl Shilton, Leicester

Fish

You can have one as a pet
Or for your dinner
You could win one at a carnival
If you're a winner!

You could keep them in a tank
Or in a bowl
You could have just one
Or an entire shoal.

You can eat cod, haddock
And even swordfish
Sardines, trout and more
And they all make a tasty dish.
So please give me more.

Michael Jordan (14)
William Bradford Community College, Earl Shilton, Leicester

9/11

Where were you when the world stopped turning, that September day?

The American public awoke in the morning
Not knowing what would become
Work, school and shopping they went
Children said bye to their mums.

Where were you when the world stopped turning, that September day?

Employees of the World Trade Centres
Made their way on up
To their office, meeting or café
Possibly to get their last cup.

Where were you when the world stopped turning, that September day?

The world stood still, to the sight of the towers
Falling to the ground
People rushing and trying to help
Staring in shock at the mound.

Where were you when the world stopped turning, that September day?

Dreadful images of the hijacked planes
Shown on national TV
People's hearts went on out
To the victims' families.

Where were you when the world stopped turning, that September day?

Shock and rage arose around
And people asking why
How could this terrible thing happen,
How were those monsters let into the sky?

Where were you when the world stopped turning, that September day?

Gavin Powers (14)
William Bradford Community College, Earl Shilton, Leicester

Dance

I walk onto the stage
To face the judges
Feeling sick and nervous
Will I bare any grudges?

The music starts
My feet move around,
I dance to the beat
And keep together with the sound.

The music stops
I go off after I have bowed
Listening to the applause,
It sounds wonderfully loud!

All the girls walk back on stage
To a tremendous applause.
We eagerly await our results
As the judge stands and gives a pause.

In reverse order
She read from her sheet
I wasn't third or second
But would I be beat?

Thankfully no!
It was all over and won!
I couldn't believe it,
I had just won!

Katie Hobbs (15)
William Bradford Community College, Earl Shilton, Leicester

Creepy Crawlies

Creepy crawlies
Are nasty things
The boys all love them
The girls all hate them.

There's a group of boys
Around a bug
One stepped down
And grabbed the vile thing.

He swung his arm
The girls all screamed
The boy threw it
It landed on a small girl.

She screamed and squirmed
Jumping up and down
Everyone looked.

The bug fell
And banged its head
It got up all dizzy and dazed
It looked at me
I looked back
Then it winked at me
I picked it up and ran inside.

I placed it on the table
Then to my surprise it said,
'Hello.'

Now I have a pet
Everyone knows
The boys all love him
The girls all hate him
Bar me 'cause I love my creepy crawly!

Katherine Moore (14)
William Bradford Community College, Earl Shilton, Leicester

Night-Time

Night-time should be a peaceful one
One that should be dark, it seems
Night-time should be quiet and motionless
But one that brings amazing dreams
Once the beautiful red sun sweeps down
From the jet-black, silent sky
The glistening, silver moon rises
And climbs way up high
Millions of tiny, twinkling gems
Watch over the sleeping town
Just like little staring eyes
The moon gleams down never sharing a frown
The darkness and silence
Covering the resting people
Like a warm, woolly blanket
Or a thick layer of treacle
The town sleeps well
With the help of a hum
From a special night-time bee
The night goes on
The flowers send out sweet, fresh smells
Everywhere is still
Curtains block out the night
Waiting for the sun to come over the hill
So shush now, hush now
Don't wake the night
Wait until the morning
So let's be quiet, quiet, quiet.

Claire Sands (14)
William Bradford Community College, Earl Shilton, Leicester

Moving Away

I'm leaving a while
I'm going away
When I come back
I'll call you, okay.

I'm leaving for a while,
I'm taking a break
If I come back,
I'm going to be late.

I'm leaving forever,
I'll never be back
If you just leave me alone
Just cut me some slack.

I'm leaving forever
But if I come back
Just leave me alone
Just cut me some slack.

Emma Barton (14)
William Bradford Community College, Earl Shilton, Leicester

Remember

Remember those risking their lives
Fighting for us, missing their wives.

Feeling sick, getting wounds
Missing their family, friends and you.

Killing, fighting and seeing friends die
Why oh why did they all have to die?

Stuck in the ground with poppies above
As doves fly around carrying love.

Jessica DeBoice (14)
William Bradford Community College, Earl Shilton, Leicester

Shopping Basket

Ouch, ouch
Not another tin of beans
Oh no!
Please!
She's putting bread in me
Oh no! Now she's coming up to the delicatessen
Cold rashers of bacon fall on my back!
Slippery, slices of ham cover me!
Next it's off to the chilled food section
Ahh! Icy cold milk drips on me
Many of my friends pass me by
Full up to the eyeballs with food!
Then I hear the screeching, the noise of the conveyor belt!
My worst enemy!
Looking like it's going to swallow me up
It's slowly turning
Sending me into a trance
Food, food, endless food
Then I wake up
Together again in a big pile
Ready for the next customer.

Claire Wragg (14)
William Bradford Community College, Earl Shilton, Leicester

Tennis

T he finals day at Wimbledon
E verybody's there, watching the final in utter silence.
N ow it's match point to the world number one
N ow it's game, set, match to Federer.
I t's the second time he's won it
S o that's it till next time, will Henman win it next year?

Ryan Perridge (14)
William Bradford Community College, Earl Shilton, Leicester

The Blurb Of My Mind

Paradise moves from place to place
Beauty changes from face to face
Emotions swing from love to hate
Why is this love always one way?

Always such a tragic end
To ordinary people love trends
Love was always lurking there
Ready to be found in the middle of nowhere
Such a waste of hard-earned feeling
And someone's mind full deep meaning.

Hearts crushed in an easy day's work
Opinions brushed like unwanted dirt
Rules and regs dished out as dinner
Media frenzies hyped up like winners
Cold, sad tears
Ran to show the fears.

Someone's dark tomb
Is another man's bright and colourful room
The control panels at rest counting sheep
As the machines at work, but also at sleep.

Lee Duffy (14)
William Bradford Community College, Earl Shilton, Leicester

Dragons

D reams and nightmares we appear in all
R ain, fire and earth we rule them all.
A ncient creatures, yes we are
G rey, black and red, we're in myths from afar.
O ften minds imagine us
N ot many now believe in us
S o many have shrivelled and died, your imagination is now no use
to us.

Ben Bartlett (14)
William Bradford Community College, Earl Shilton, Leicester

Big Mistake

We woke up,
Took a day off school,
Went on a shopping spree,
Thought we were cool,
The first place we went,
Was a big toy store,
Got something small,
Wanted more,
The next place we went,
Was a jewellery shop,
Took something else,
Just couldn't stop,
After that,
It was a piece of cake,
The last shop we went in,
Was a big mistake,
We were so good,
Well that's what we thought,
We were about to leave,
Then we got caught.

The rush you get,
From the risks you take,
Just isn't worth it
What a big mistake.

Jade Richards (14)
William Bradford Community College, Earl Shilton, Leicester

What Is Love?

What is love? Is it a feeling or is it a sign, or is it an object you cry over
or pine?
Is it paper that declares your love, or is it the ring under your left hand's
glove?
What do you do when you are in love, do you hold hands, cuddle or
hug?
This I'm afraid is up to you, how you react when you say I do!

Sophie Sherwin (14)
William Bradford Community College, Earl Shilton, Leicester

Animal Cruelty

Some will use a stick
Some will use a hammer
But at the end of the day
Does it really matter?
It's all the same, it's inhumane.

Drugs and beatings
Pills and punches
Pain and misery
Who are the animals?
Them or us?

We take their freedom
Maim, mistreat them
How can we justify?
It's such a shame, it's inhumane
Can't we hear their desperate cry?

Daniel Hone (14)
William Bradford Community College, Earl Shilton, Leicester

Love Is . . .

Love is like a rose,
Delicate,
          Fragile hearts can break
Rosy red,
          Cheeks are blushing innocently.
Thorny,
          Broken hearts will hurt
Attractive,
          Just one glance and you're addicted.
But overall,
          It's blooming marvellous!

Laura Whitehouse (14)
William Bradford Community College, Earl Shilton, Leicester

Don't Annoy Me

To annoy someone, is to anger someone
And to anger me is to kick a bee's hive
The buzzing of their voice
Stinging in my ear
They fly around me, just waiting for me to snap
Like a weak ruler
Buzz, buzz, buzz
I start to shake
Buzz, buzz, buzz
I'm starting to sweat!
The yellow followed by the black, followed by yellow, followed by
black.

The hive, they're kicking my hive, the bees fly out
And they're stinging me, inside my head
To annoy me is to kick a bee's hive
And to kick a bee's hive, means trouble.

Natalie Foster (14)
William Bradford Community College, Earl Shilton, Leicester

Man City

Man City are the best
They're better than all the rest
They always make me smile
When Anelka scores from a mile.

Kevin Keegan is the best
David James is a pest
Sun-Ji Hai runs one mile
Anelka seems to always smile
Sean Wright-Phillips scores a goal
To make it 4-1 to Man City.

Jake Hardman (15)
William Bradford Community College, Earl Shilton, Leicester

From Under The Bed

The doorknob turned
I froze with fear
Praying he wouldn't notice me hiding here;
Under the bed,
That's where I lay,
Hoping he would just go away
I saw his knife shine,
His feet entered the room,
My breath started to quiver,
I knew my doom.
But then to my luck,
After stalking the floor
He turned right around

And walked out of the door.

Nichola Birtwisle (14)
William Bradford Community College, Earl Shilton, Leicester

Love!

Love . . . well how can I describe it?
It's a feeling that you find bit by bit,
He's the best, I hear you say,
You've only known him for a day.

When you see him walk in the room,
You say to me your heart goes boom.
You talk about him all the time,
That's why I am now writing this rhyme.

Love . . . I just described it.

Hannah Butler (14)
William Bradford Community College, Earl Shilton, Leicester

Life As A Soldier

Left, right, left, right
Trying hard with all my might
'Come on boys, over the top.'
Up we go, just to be shot
Men get stuck in the barbed wire
Breathing in gas, acting on fire
Down we go to the enemy trench
Running past lads dying on a bench
Bayonets in
A terrible sin
Men scream and shout
Floundering all about
Now I am asleep
Lying dead.

Philip Page (14)
William Bradford Community College, Earl Shilton, Leicester

Friendship

Friends are angels
Sent from above,
Always there for you,
Sharing their love.

The best kind of friend,
Is the one you trust
The one you have fun with,
The one who is just.

My great friends
Are the best,
Fun, happy and caring,
Better than all the rest.

Kirsty Everton (15)
William Bradford Community College, Earl Shilton, Leicester

All The Love

All the love that's in my heart
It's special and it's rare
It will always be for you
It's tender like a teddy bear.

All the love that's in my heart
I've held it for quite a while
I will do anything for you
Even run ten thousand miles.

All the love that's in my heart
Hopes we never part
Because the love forever remains
Kept inside my heart.

Kelsey Starkey (14)
William Bradford Community College, Earl Shilton, Leicester

Love

We walked in the cold
You held my frozen hand
I felt like I was worth a grand.

We walked to the park
Before it turned dark,
And shared a kiss.

It was bliss
I woke from a dream
Realised where I've been.

Cara Ellis (14)
William Bradford Community College, Earl Shilton, Leicester

Love Is

Love is a moonlight walk along a sun kissed beach
Love is a beautiful red rose on Valentine's day
Love is knowing that you're always there for me when I need you
Love is your hand linked to mine.

Love is a passionate kiss from me to you
Love is a little bit of romance every now and then
Love is something that should be cherished
Love is between covers.

Love is a feeling from deep within your heart
Love is breakfast in bed from a special someone
Love is me and you together until the end
Love is walking under the stars.

Laura Watkins (14)
William Bradford Community College, Earl Shilton, Leicester

Motorbikes

M otor bikes are really good,
O il and petrol mixed with mud.
T rials and motocross is what I enjoy,
E arly age I learn, oh boy.
R eady steady, here I go,
B rakes, brakes, the fluid level's low.
I n the air off the ramp,
K eep on wishing it was not so damp.
E ngine blows from all the strain,
S tupid bike, what a pain.

Kirby Neale (14)
William Bradford Community College, Earl Shilton, Leicester

Possession

I grip the arms of my chair,
As the pain rattles my insides.
As the tears tumble down my face,
My screams get louder and louder,
The walls around me fading away,
Every last scream,
Gets quieter,
Eerier,
The memories are still vivid,
Like they happened yesterday,
The blood,
The looks of horror,
The sirens and flashing lights,
The sweat pours down my face,
And mingles with the tears
My fears are still with me,
Every time I hear his voice,
Beckoning me to do the things I hate
To sin,
To join in him death,
I fight and scream,
Using every last breath to resist,
But it's becoming so hard,
His voice is whispering,
'Pick up the blade,
Pick up the blade,'
I sob and scream
And bounce off the walls,
Just to stop the voice,
The blood,
My blood,
Has been shed too many times,
It's time to move on,
To let me rest,

The rope smells like paradise,
I close my eyes and count to 3,
I let out my final cry
'This is for you.'

Emma Mockett (14)
William Bradford Community College, Earl Shilton, Leicester

Painful Passion

Love is like a gunshot
It makes you feel like you have lost the plot
It hits you when you are least expecting it
Bang
Should you let your love go?
What should you do?
Have you lost the plot?
Have you been shot?

When your love is near
It feels like a fear
Your head goes crazy
Your stomach goes queer
That's how you know your love is near.

Despite all this fear
You love him
And that's what he wants to hear
Even though your stomach goes queer
You love him!
Love hurts like Heaven and Hell
But you think your love will go well.

You now like the pain
And you know you have gained
What you have never had before
So I should hope you would never walk out that old door!

Gemma Quinney (14)
William Bradford Community College, Earl Shilton, Leicester

What To Do?

Wednesday in room 2
I don't know what to do
I haven't got a clue
My friend has some glue
Though how that helps, I just don't know!
So I still don't know what to do!

If I don't get this done
I won't spend lunch in the sun
Then I might have to run
To catch the bus numbered 101
But still I don't know what to do!

Tomorrow I won't have a clue
Of what I am meant to do
I'll never ever know what I was supposed to do
Oh well, boo-hoo.

Arthur Pigou & Chris Fisher (14)
William Bradford Community College, Earl Shilton, Leicester

Where?

I looked east and west and they
Still haven't come.

I stayed there day and night but,
They still didn't come.

Backwards and forwards I went down that road
And nobody still had come.

I asked certain ladies and gentlemen who walked past,
Somehow
I don't think they will come.

Matthew Thornton (14)
William Bradford Community College, Earl Shilton, Leicester

Poem About Friends

F riends are loyal
R eliable
I nteresting and fun
E specially kind
N ice to you
D ear to the heart
S ecrets are kept.

F unny
O nly person to confide in
R eally special
E ver lasting
V irtually family
E xtremely loyal
R are to find.

Danielle Thorne (14)
William Bradford Community College, Earl Shilton, Leicester

Fish

Fish, what does it mean?
Slimy, scaly, wet
Salmon, carp or pet
Ocean, river or lake
Fry, batter or bake
Tail, fins and scales
Goldfish, dolphins or whales
Wet pet, wet friend, wet feast
Small, large or beast
Fish, what does it mean?

Oliver Broad (15)
William Bradford Community College, Earl Shilton, Leicester

An Old Man Of 85

At the age of 85 I am not an old man
Is that what you see?
I am not the old fool that you think I may be
My bones are weak and my hair is grey, but
Can't you see I'm still here today!
I fought with my fellows during the war and
Some awful sights I saw
I sat by the old mill lake eating cake after cake
Whilst catching fishes galore!
I was young once with spare time on my hands
In my shed I would sit and wonder why
The world flashes so quickly by.
I made sledges for my young
And brought presents for my wife
As I look back at my life,
These hands of mine so weak and fragile
Is that what you see when you look at me?
These withered old hands, are the hands of a work man
Powerful and strong.
I tell you now, I am not an old man,
I am a war hero, a war hero captured,
Destined to escape from this broken down body.

Amy Cox (14)
William Bradford Community College, Earl Shilton, Leicester

Don't Come Last

Bang!
There goes the gun, time to go, time to run.
Get off the blocks extra fast,
To make sure that I don't come last.
I drive with my arms
I push with my legs
I'm sprinting now,
Really fast . . .
To make sure that I don't come last.

Amy Mitchell (14)
William Bradford Community College, Earl Shilton, Leicester

Cupid

He strung up his bow and arrow
Stepped forward to see the world below his cloud
He thought of all the memories
All of the people he'd made happy
And the times he gave to others
That's all he gave: love, time, memories, treasures.

Cupid was tired and hungry for something in return
Something he had dealt in for many a-century
The one thing he did not receive himself . . .
Love.

His pink cloud darkened,
Shadows lurked, forcing their way through his mind
He cried and sobbed and begged
He pleaded and clutched his empty heart through his soul . . .
But it did not beat.

Hatred grew over countries
Life began to weaken,
People battled, fought and threw back any existence of compassion
for each other.

Cupid was unemployed over grief and agony
He became blind through no blindfold
Cupid died
Only the ones he blessed before, lived and tried to remember
A time when love was living.

Kim Domican (15)
William Bradford Community College, Earl Shilton, Leicester

Bob And His Dog

There was a young man called Bob
Who hit his head on a log
He started to cry
So he wiped his eyes dry
And carried on looking for his dog.

Ashley Woodley (14)
William Bradford Community College, Earl Shilton, Leicester

Hit And Run

Good night out with the lads
Drank a few beers
Fell over a bar stool
Got a few cheers.

Fell over in the car park
Landed on my knees
Rummaged in my pockets
Somehow found my keys.

Got into my car, head spinning
Switched on the radio, United winning?

Speeding down the road
Flying past the trees
Rooftop down
Late night breeze.

He stepped out in front of me!
I couldn't find the brake!
He rolled over the bonnet!
It was a mistake!

No one saw it, I could just go home?
But that could be someone's father, husband, son
Lying in the road?

I saw it in the paper
Father of four dies
My wife saw the bumper, asked me what I'd hit
'A dog,' I lied

It was the funeral today
Everybody cried
James was a good mate
Shame he went and died . . .

Matt Lawrenson (14)
William Bradford Community College, Earl Shilton, Leicester

Blank

A spark of inspiration
That's what I'm waiting for;
To write a little poem
Of about twelve lines or more.

You see I have a feeling
A tiny part of me
It's calling out quite loudly
For me to set it free.

I'm not sure what it's saying
It's quite confusing really
If there was something wrong
It would tell me . . . surely?

It confuses me completely
Turns me upside down
Makes my whole world spin
Twists my head around!

It speaks to me gently
It yells into my ear
I can always listen
But I can never hear.

It's not a daily occurrence
Just now and then it's true!
But when I've had an odd day
I wonder . . . do you have that feeling too?

Nina Marvin (14)
William Bradford Community College, Earl Shilton, Leicester

Friends

Friends are the people we go to
When we are sad, happy or depressed.
They're a shoulder to cry on
Or just someone to have a laugh with.
Friends are the best.

Hannah Maloney (14)
William Bradford Community College, Earl Shilton, Leicester

Why I Love Fashion

I love fashion
It's fun
It's funky
And it's colourful
There are all different makes, sizes and prices.
Shop for shoes, bags and clothes.
Shop till you drop.
Buy summer bikinis
Winter jumpers
Pointy shoes and not to forget those mini skirts
Fashion comes in, fashion goes out,
From season to season
From colour to colour
From pattern to pattern
And to the catwalk and back.

Kaitlin Duckworth (14)
William Bradford Community College, Earl Shilton, Leicester

Dad

I thought Daddy was only playing,
When he locked me in my room.

I thought Daddy was only playing,
When he swore and shouted at me.

I thought Daddy was only playing,
When I cried, but he just turned away.

I knew Daddy wasn't playing,
When he swung and hit me.

Now I know Daddy isn't playing,
So I'm in my room crying and still he turns away.

Paige Steane (14)
William Bradford Community College, Earl Shilton, Leicester

Careless

Tears stream on an angelic face
A face full of shame and disgrace
She didn't ask for this
She just yearns for true love's kiss
She tried to show she could care
But no one noticed, it wasn't fair.
She felt like an outcast
And all she wanted was a love that would last
She didn't want to be alone
Just searching for a place to call home
She wished that she could escape
She didn't want to feel this hate
She wanted to fly away
And maybe return another day
But until that day, the tears she will cry
A love burning inside, that just won't die.

Sophie Gent (14)
William Bradford Community College, Earl Shilton, Leicester

Fear

There it was to my surprise
The terror flowing through my eyes
Above my head it slowly fluttered
Unable to move I silently suffered
All of a sudden my legs broke free
I ran out of the room immediately
Up the stairs, down the hall
Tripping on my sister's ball.
Reaching my room I collapsed on the bed
Panting like a dog, I wiped my head
I slowly sat up peering through the door
Didn't stand up until I was sure
The moth had gone through the window
I slammed it shut with one swift flow.

Amy Lymn (14)
William Bradford Community College, Earl Shilton, Leicester

The Night After

It was the night after the last,
Nearly all day had past
The sweet cherries were still sticky on the table
She is woken by the slight pitter of rain
That was silence to the dormouse that downstairs in the corridor
She pulls the covers back and slides out of bed
She puts on her make-up and brushes her hair
So every strand is standing fair
She runs down stairs as fast as she can
To see if the milkman has been.
Bang! A gunshot is fired, blood runs down the step
Where it is washed away by the rain.
There was no longer silence in the air
But horrific screams.
She sleeps peacefully again, never to be woken,
By the pitter of rain.

Yvette Aspin (14)
William Bradford Community College, Earl Shilton, Leicester

Me And My Friend

Always standing by to help
    You through your day
Holding you up when you are feeling
    Weak . . .

Catching the tears that are going around
    Pulling you through
The tough parts of
    Life . . .

Standing by when you are
    Feeling low
Trying to make you laugh
    When you are going through tough times.

All I want to say is you are my friend.

Ashleigh Newell (14)
William Bradford Community College, Earl Shilton, Leicester

Devil's Day

I am standing at the gates of Hell
With the decaying and the charcoal smell
Demented creatures coming towards me
Standing in front of me, the Devil, the 'He'
He says to me, 'For you I have plans,'
Upon my face His twisted and bony hands.

All of a sudden a bright white light
Astonished by a terrible sight
This brought thought to my suspicion
I was on a deadly mission.
There it was
My teacher, the Devil
Beside me sat a quaking Neville.

A brief moment in time,
12 struck the clock of a chime
My time of peace started by the bell
Stopped my moment in Hell
Enchanted by this spell.

Helen Mayne (15)
William Bradford Community College, Earl Shilton, Leicester

Sophie

Sophie is my little sister, she is as happy as can be
She is a little sweetie
She will soon be six years old and is excited for her party
With all her little friends
I am not allowed to go
I will stay with Dad
I'm really glad for my little sister
And hope she will be really happy.

James Sweeney (14)
William Bradford Community College, Earl Shilton, Leicester

Why Did It Have To Be Him?

Standing alone, isolated,
Surrounded only by his own great layers of fat
Why did it have to be him?

Always last to be picked for any team that
Was chosen by his peers,
Why did it have to be him?

Eating his dinner alone,
Lonely even in a great crowd of people,
Why did it have to be him?

'Choose a partner, we're working in pairs today.'
Those words always echoed around his head and made him panic
Why did it have to be him?

The one who nobody wanted to be near
The one who received all the snide comments
Why did it have to be him?

Didn't they know how he felt?
Left out and ridiculed at every opportunity?
Why did it have to be him?

Mallory Thorpe (14)
William Bradford Community College, Earl Shilton, Leicester

Happiness

Happiness is the glitter in an eye
Happiness is the smile on a face
Happiness is the sound of music
Happiness is the smell of flowers
Happiness is the sweet taste of chocolate
Happiness is knowing you have friends
Happiness is the sound of laughing
Happiness is having fun - are you happy?
Happiness is the scent of roses - I am!

Laura Houghton (14)
William Bradford Community College, Earl Shilton, Leicester

Vampire

The blood drips from her neck
The claws scrape across the door
The next night he looks at his next victim in awe
As she screams, his fangs sink into her flesh
She falls silent to the floor.

The vampire returns to his coffin
As the day breaks
They find her on the floor
Her eyes now empty and lifeless.

The next night they hunt him
Waiting for him to strike
And catch him as his fangs sink into her neck.
They make a cross he turns and runs.

They follow him to the graveyard
And all the way to a crypt
They open the coffins until only one is left
They prise the lid open and look inside
His body is pink and fresh-like; he died yesterday
They drive the stake through his chest
He moans and then turns to ash
The curse is broken, or so they believe
As a shadowy figure slips through the mist.

Mathew Smith (14)
William Bradford Community College, Earl Shilton, Leicester

Signs

Signs on the road
Signs in my heart
A sign telling me what's
There and what's not
Signed on the line
Just for you
So please be true.

Siobhan Hanson-Spence (14)
William Bradford Community College, Earl Shilton, Leicester

Daddy Loves Us

She sits in a dark corner,
Awaiting the cries from her mother
Scared of her father and trapped in the walls he's built around her,
Cold, wet tears running down her bruised face,
As she watches her father's fist put her mother in her place,
She tries so hard to block out the pain,
But all she is thinking is that the bruises will fade
The screams suddenly stop,
Silence is ahead,
He picks up her mother and throws her on the bed,
He spots her
His piercing eyes are burning through her
He picks up his shirt
He goes off to work
It's over for tonight
But there her mother lay
But it will be ok
One day . . .

Laura Di Salvo (15)
William Bradford Community College, Earl Shilton, Leicester

The Everyday Life Of The Average Hamster

H oping to get out, hoping to be played with before they go to bed
A round and around in my wheel.
M mm, hamster pellets
S lump around my cage for a while
T ear and chew at the door a bit
E at that treat they pushed through the bars when they woke up
R est and start over again.

Holly Beasley (14)
William Bradford Community College, Earl Shilton, Leicester

The Charge

Along the line of flame and fire
Stand the men in mud and mire
So they stand brothers in arms
Through the drone of the alarms.
Their faces set with grim dire
Eyes betray their pain and tire
Shells they fall all around
Making deaf who hear their sound.
Once the guns stop their barrage
The men of valance and hope they charge
Lines of men run over the hill
The enemy ready for the kill.
Though fight they did with tooth and nail
Their fateful charge was doomed to fail
Five hundred their number, five hundred stories told
Each one of them noble, each one of them bold.

Billy Mitchell (14)
William Bradford Community College, Earl Shilton, Leicester

Pollution

P is for power stations polluting the air
O is for damaging the o-zone layer
L is for litter thrown onto the ground
L is for loud noises heard all around
U is for uncontrollable dumping in seas
T is for acid rain's threat to trees
 I is for illegal dumping of waste
O is for oil the fish can taste
N is for nothing, no trees only soil,
     This is what will happen if you keep dumping oil.

Nicola-May Mangham (14)
William Bradford Community College, Earl Shilton, Leicester

Eclipse

The wolf calls out to the moon
It will be here soon
It will be here,
Shadows whisper in the trees
Footsteps padding with the breeze
It will be here soon,
It will be here,
Something stretches through the wood tonight
Darkness will cover every bit of light
It will be here soon
It will be here,
The lonely wolf cries to the moon
To see if it will try and bloom
Finally it has begun.
With red in the sky and light nearly gone
Just then the Earth is cast aside
As the sun fights for its right in the sky.
Moon in the middle, Earth at the end
Will the sun ever shine again?
Then in the middle of the wood
A flash appears, the deed is done
The moon disappears.

Hayley Billington (14)
William Bradford Community College, Earl Shilton, Leicester

Homework

I was asked to write a poem
And didn't have a clue
For days and days I wondered
What could I do?
Then I had an idea and gave it a shot
I worked at it till it was done
And this is what I got.

Katie Middleton (14)
William Bradford Community College, Earl Shilton, Leicester

I Was Told To Write A Poem

I was told to write a poem
But I'm not really that good
I thought I'd give it a go
If I tried hard, I could.

I wasn't sure how to start it
I needed it to be catching
My brain started ticking
And ideas started hatching.

The middle wasn't too hard
It wasn't really that bad
I had some help you see
From my mate and his dad.

The ending was the easiest part
It was really simple to write.
I think I'll go to bed now
So auf wiedersehen, goodnight.

Tom Holdsworth (14)
William Bradford Community College, Earl Shilton, Leicester

The Bloody War

Being in the war is so sad,
No one ever dreamed it could be this bad,
I miss my family and my friends
The attacking keeps on going it never ends,
Fighting for my country I was meant to be proud,
But the hurt and the pain continues, the crying is so loud,
Please let me return home I can't stand anymore,
I wish I wasn't involved in this bloody war.

Adelle Armstrong (14)
William Bradford Community College, Earl Shilton, Leicester

Me And My Dream

The bright light you saw
Was nothing more
The hope you had
Has now gone back
The dream you dreamed
Was nothing more than it seemed
It felt so right that night
Up on stage in my own spotlight
I want to be a star
I really do
I've come this far
And then I wake up
It's over now
It's not fair
But you'll see me soon somewhere.

Robyn Mains (14)
William Bradford Community College, Earl Shilton, Leicester

Butterflies

A stranger
        You are
    As you step upon my doorstep
I left you behind
    To start fresh
        You had wiped the slate clean
    Yet now you return to me?
Am I supposed to take you back?
    Am I supposed to forgive you
        For all you did to me?
    Yet as I look into your eyes
            My knees begin to buckle
                    I get butterflies
    Just as I always did.

Jessie White (14)
William Bradford Community College, Earl Shilton, Leicester

Nothing Hurts . . .

I lie awake at night
Waiting for a bright light
One to remove me from the dark hole
This place hurts so bad
Sucking away all the happiness I once had.
What have I done to deserve this pain?
My heart constantly rains.
The tears flow and trickle down my face
One day this pain will end
This is just a learning bend
I will take this lesson to my grave
Nothing hurts as much as love.

Sarah Harding (14)
William Bradford Community College, Earl Shilton, Leicester

Hamster

Hamster
Hamster
I have a hamster
I pick him up, I pick him up
He bites me on my thumb
'Oh no, oh no,' I said
I clean him out
I clean him out
He crawled up my arm, down my trousers
He tickles, he tickles, he tickles so much
He makes me laugh so loud,
That my dad says
'Shut up!'

Charlotte Grewcock (14)
William Bradford Community College, Earl Shilton, Leicester

Bullied Mind

There we were eye to eye
People shouting fight, fight, fight
I saw a tear running down his face
So I whacked him, he looked a disgrace
He went to the floor like a sack of spuds
I kicked him in the face with an echoing thud
Later that day a teacher came
Looking furious, mad, looking at the boy in pain
I then got home, my mum asked me why
I sighed and began to cry
Later that night I thought, *what was the point?*
He made me angry and annoyed
Now he knows not to mess with me
I'm not your favourite cup of tea.

Scott Christopher (14)
William Bradford Community College, Earl Shilton, Leicester

Mysterious Eyes

Does she know that I can see her?
I know that she can see me.
For days she has wandered behind me,
Watching, always watching.
Is she following me?
Is she looking into the future?
Is she staring into the past?
Is she there at all?

Adam Farmer (14)
William Bradford Community College, Earl Shilton, Leicester

Fair Trade

Stood on my feet
On the dried brown soil
Working in the fields all day long.

Rain or shine,
Whether I'm ill or well
Working in the fields all day long.

Tiny grains of rice,
I pick for a living
Working in the fields all day long.

To feed my family
Every single day
Working in the fields all day.

Emily Bates (14)
William Bradford Community College, Earl Shilton, Leicester

Friends

Can we be friends or not?
I've asked you twice, but you seem to have *forgot!*
Please tell me now so I can see,
Whether we are still friends to be.
Of all the friends I've had or met,
You're the one I wouldn't forget.
I hope our friendship will forever last
So let's just make up and forget the past.

Rebecca Gault (14)
William Bradford Community College, Earl Shilton, Leicester

Friends

They are there when you laugh
And there when you cry
There through your lows
And there through your highs
They can give excellent advice
And can read you like a book
If you want friends just like this
All you have to do is look.

Kirsty Grewcock (14)
William Bradford Community College, Earl Shilton, Leicester

Dream Man

Dream man, where are you?
Really want to meet you
Every day I think of you
At night I am without you
My very own dream man.

My dreams could become a reality,
And when I am with you, I will
Never let you go.

Florence Powers (14)
William Bradford Community College, Earl Shilton, Leicester

Bullies!

I hate bullies they're horrible to me
They make out they're bigger and better than me
They hurt everyone, kick and hit.
Don't forget they even spit.
Then all of a sudden it goes quiet and I think to myself what have I
done?

Emma Hogg (14)
William Bradford Community College, Earl Shilton, Leicester

Classroom

Children around you, talking
Loud,
Abusive language.
Sounds of every kind, books slamming, teachers
Shouting.
'Right children, stop talking,' the teacher shouts.
'Ow no, I ain't stopping,' the kid answered back!
'Out, get out,' the teacher was mad.
Mood changed drastically, no more talking, it had ended.

Todd Astill (14)
William Bradford Community College, Earl Shilton, Leicester

Food

Fish and chips
Pork pies
All adds to the weight of my thighs.

Iced buns
Cream cake
All of which my mum can make.

Food, food
Food galore
All this food I want more.

Ben Lester (14)
William Bradford Community College, Earl Shilton, Leicester

What Is Happiness?

Happiness is love at first sight,
Happiness is having a good night,
Happiness is friends that care,
Happiness is people that are always there,
Happiness is fun and laughter,
Happiness is happy ever after.

Laura Crowe-Denoon (14)
William Bradford Community College, Earl Shilton, Leicester

That Stupid Ref!

That stupid ref
Needs to go to Specsavers
That surely was a goal
By that super Arsenal player!

The whistle goes!
1-1, oh no!
Extra time - here goes
Portugal are attacking
Come on defenders, get tackling,
Goal to Portugal
Rui Costa!
How I hate him.

Lampard saved us
Brought us back
Into the game
So here comes
The dreaded penalties.

Please Sven
Don't let Becks go first
So up steps the egg head
The country groans.

He places the ball
Chooses his target
40 feet up into the sky!

The country's pride falls
Cursing him!
Unlucky Vassel,
Not your fault,
It was the egghead that aimed for the sky.

Matt Palmer-Rowe (14)
William Bradford Community College, Earl Shilton, Leicester

The Theme Park

The bar comes down
With a loud clunk
And now my heart
Begins to thump
I look at my friend
She looks back at me
I feel so scared
And I need a wee
A loud whirring starts
Somewhere down low
My friend looks at me
What's happening now?
A long low creak
And the ride begins
'Let me out!'
A woman sings
My heart thumped so hard
I thought it might burst
Surely it wouldn't
Get much worse?
We get moving
With quite a slow start
But I was still thinking
About my poor heart
Faster and faster
Round we go
We go up high
Then come down low
We grind to a halt and my friend looks at me
I look back, smile, and then . . . we go again!

Rebecca Fisher (14)
William Bradford Community College, Earl Shilton, Leicester

Love

Love is like the air that we breathe
Love is like the world that we see,
Love chokes like a nuclear bomb.
Love makes you feel like you can't go on,
Love can be a beautiful thing
Love makes you want to stand up and sing
Love is the best when it's shared with another
Love is the worst when you have no lover
        Love's like fire
        Never stops burning!

Rachael Pole (14)
William Bradford Community College, Earl Shilton, Leicester

The Dragon's Mind

Do you think we are afraid of you?
You think we're mythical, you haven't a clue
We could rise from the sand,
To reclaim our land,
We live forever in fear of elves,
But now you can't defend yourselves
We'll rule again just you see
And now you know you can't beat me!

Christopher Liston (14)
William Bradford Community College, Earl Shilton, Leicester

We Will Win

E xcitement when they kick the ball
N ever give up, you're playing for them all,
G rass under your feet been cut, ready to play
L oud and proud the crowd are today
A rmies of fans come into the ground
N ervous waiting for the whistle to sound
D o it for your country, do it for them all!

Brett Chambers (14)
William Bradford Community College, Earl Shilton, Leicester

Easter Time

Easter is a special time
So I am writing a little rhyme
The Easter bunny with his basket full
The spring lambs in the hillside with lots of wool
Chocolate eggs for me to eat
The farmer with his harvest wheat
The child with no Easter treat begs
Longing for some chocolate eggs
At school we had an Easter collection
For lonely children within our section.

Natalie Bedder (14)
William Bradford Community College, Earl Shilton, Leicester

Broken Love

I thought you liked her
Now I know you do
Why did you bother to lie to me
I know that isn't you.

I don't like playing games
I thought you didn't too
So why did you do that to me
When you knew my heart was true?

Jemma Bradley (15)
William Bradford Community College, Earl Shilton, Leicester

Summer

S ummer days and summer nights
U nder the parasol keeping cool,
M errily taking a paddle,
M aybe a little swim
E ating ice creams along the shore
R aring to go out for a little bit more!

Naomi Henson (14)
William Bradford Community College, Earl Shilton, Leicester

My Dream Was True

Warm it was, the summer day before
A faint light tapping came tapping at my door
Mother glided in and asked if I was alright
I said that I was fine, kissed and said goodnight.

I drifted off to a peaceful dream
Or so I thought 'cause that's how it seemed
Then a fairy flew right into my room
She came so fast you could hear the zoom.

Bringing a burst of sweet, warm air
She was pretty and blue with the most perfect hair
She looked like a model from a magazine
She had the best figure I had ever seen.

We glided away, my clothes suddenly changed
To a silver ballroom gown of the best range
We flew to a beautiful ballroom do
We landed down and off she flew.

I entered in, the whole room stared
As I carried on walking down the stairs
Everyone turned and went back to their thing
In the background you could hear the opera sing.

I stood there feeling funny all over
A boy asked my name, I said it was Clover
'That is very pretty,' he answered back
He bowed quite low and took off his hat.

He took my hand, then kissed it with care
We danced for an hour with gaze and stare
Dancing so swift like a prince and a princess
The light made the stuff glitter from my dress.

We walked into the moonlight, standing under the stars
We kissed so sweetly the moon said, 'Aaahhh.'
We were in love, you could see it from the start
The most magical feeling was in my heart.

We swapped each other's numbers
We promised to call
It felt like flying, like being ten feet tall
We kissed once more and went back into the room
The clock went chime then I heard a fast zoom.

The alarm clock went beep
I was lying in a heap
I woke up thinking, 'It was only a dream',
But with the window open it was a funny scene.

My phone rang, I picked it up
I heard his voice, my heart went thump
We talked for ages, then I put it on charge
I know he is my love, it is just there in my heart.

A piece of paper was in my hand
I saw the number and only realised just that
My dream was true!

Shanice Coy (12)
Woodfield Middle School, Redditch

We Are The Brackets

(Inspired by 'I Am A Full Stop' by Derek Stuart)

We are the brackets
We hold extra information in our hands
We can be squared and also curved
Sentences can do without us
But we make life so much more interesting.

We are the speech marks
We surround the words you say
We make your words come alive
Ignore us
And you will be speechless.

Khadeja Tulkabara & Rebecca Makin (12)
Woodfield Middle School, Redditch

I Am A Comma

(Inspired by 'I Am A Full Stop' by Derek Stuart)

I am a comma
On my demand everything separates.
You will be in danger unless you pause
Put me in the wrong place
I can change the meaning
Learn to control me
And you'll have breathing space.

I am a question mark
When I appear
I demand answers.
Who, what, when, where, why
Are worthless without me
When I appear everything is clear
What would you do without me?

I am an exclamation mark!
I shout and scream!
Without me a dramatic phrase
Is simply nothing
Without me
There is no excitement
Forget me at your peril!

Jason Hopkins & Adeel Nasir (12)
Woodfield Middle School, Redditch